How to Select TOP-PERFORMING MUTUAL FUND INVESTMENTS

Aaron H. Coleman and David H. Coleman

International Information Associates, Inc.
Morrisville, Pennsylvania

Library of Congress Number: 93-77638

Coleman, Aaron H. and David H. Coleman

ISBN 0-945510-14-4

International Information Associates, Inc.
P.O. Box 773, Morrisville, PA 19067-0773 U.S.A.

Current printing [last digit]:

10 9 8 7 6 5 4 3 2 1

Printed in the United States of America

Table of Contents

What the Book is About

This book describes a four-step process for selecting top-performing mutual fund investment systems. Such systems are a combination of a top-performing market timing model (or system) and an associated growth fund selection method. The selection process described has been developed during the past seven years by the authors as part of the Association of Mutual Fund Investors (AMFI). AMFI is a nonprofit corporation devoted to mutual fund investment research and education. Before 1993, AMFI operated as the Mutual Fund Special Interest Group (MFG) of the AAII Philadelphia Chapter.

To select the 1993 top-performing investment systems, the authors determined the five top-performing market timing models from 45 candidates. The determination was based upon the 5-year performance of the S&P 500 Index when timed by the candidate models. Then, we used our growth fund selection method to determine the best growth fund when each top-performing model generated a Buy signal. We then computed the hypothetical performance of the five top-performing investment systems during the 11-year period from 1982 through 1992. The top-performing investment system achieved a compounded rate of return of **38%** as compared to **17%** for the S&P 500 Index during that same 11-year period.

Any serious individual investor can learn how to invest his/her assets using the investment methods described in this book. He/she can also do so by participating in an AMFI chapter.

1: INTRODUCTION

Overview

This book describes how an individual investor can select top-performing mutual fund investment systems for use in achieving substantial long-term growth of his/her assets. The information presented is based upon the results of investment research conducted by the authors at the Association of Mutual Fund Investors (AMFI). AMFI, an independent, nonprofit corporation, assists mutual fund investors to become effective managers of their invested assets by conducting programs of investment research, education and information dissemination.

We have written this report for individual investors with investment background and experience ranging from zero to ten, on a scale of ten. To facilitate our communication with all potential readers, we have included investment fundamentals in Chapter 2 and a glossary of investment terms in Appendix A.

The authors, and the publisher, do not make any investment recommendations in this book nor do they assume any responsibility for the accuracy of the information presented. Furthermore, the authors, and the publishers, do not claim nor imply that historical data necessarily has a relevance to the future performance of the overall stock market, individual mutual funds or mutual fund investment systems.

What is a Mutual Fund Investment System?

A mutual fund investment system (See Table 1) is a precisely defined investment methodology that is usually implemented on a personal computer. The basics are shown in Table 1. The system preserves capital by transferring assets to a money market fund in anticipation of, and during periods when stock prices are falling. The system achieves capital growth by transferring assets to a common stock or (growth) mutual fund in anticipation of (and during) periods when stock prices are increasing.

In other words, assets are switched from a growth fund to a money market fund or vice versa according to a market timing, or ***mktime*** model or subsystem.

TABLE 1
WHAT IS A MUTUAL FUND INVESTMENT SYSTEM ?

1. A PRECISELY DEFINED METHODOLOGY THAT:

   ☐ IS USUALLY IMPLEMENTED ON A PERSONAL COMPUTER

   ☐ SWITCHES ASSETS FROM A STOCK (OR GROWTH) FUND TO A MONEY MARKET FUND AND VICE VERSA

   ☐ CONSISTS OF TWO COMPONENTS:
   - MARKET TIMING (MKTIME) MODEL
   - GROWTH FUND SELECTION SYSTEM

2. A MKTIME MODEL GENERATES BUY AND SELL SIGNALS

   ☐ WHEN A BUY SIGNAL IS GENERATED, ASSETS ARE INVESTED OR TRANSFERRED INTO A GROWTH FUND

   ☐ WHEN A SELL SIGNAL IS GENERATED, ASSETS ARE INVESTED OR TRANSFERRED INTO A MONEY MARKET FUND.

3. A GROWTH FUND SELECTION SYSTEM SELECTS THE BEST GROWTH FUND FOR INVESTMENT WHEN A BUY SIGNAL IS GENERATED.

Such an investment system consists of two parts:

- The ***mktime model*** that generates Buy or Sell signals. A Buy signal indicates that assets should be invested in or transferred into a growth fund. A Sell signal indicates that the opposite action should be executed; namely, assets should be invested or transferred into a money market fund.
- The ***growth fund selection system*** that selects the best growth fund for investment when a Buy signal is generated.

Why is a Long-Term-Growth Investment Program Necessary?

As indicated in Table 2, the objective of a long-term-growth investment program is to achieve substantial growth of one's invested assets (after adjustment for inflation and income taxes) during a period of five or more years. To increase the value of an investment, after adjustments for inflation and income taxes, the gross annual return of such investment must be greater than 7.1% based upon the assumptions shown in Table 2. As indicated in Table 3, a long-term-growth investment program is essential in today's economic climate to achieve such goals as a comfortable retirement, and the college education of children and grandchildren.

Such an investment program is essential for achieving a comfortable standard-of-living during a typical retirement period of 15 or more years because:

- No American can count on the Social Security program to provide more income than the poverty-line income. The ***maximum*** annual social security income that an individual retiring in 1992 will receive is approximately $13,000.
- Most company pensions do not provide for inflation (or cost-of-living) adjustments after retirement. Since most Americans will live at least 15 years after retiring at age 65, their inflation-adjusted pension income will have dropped to one-half its initial value at the end of the 15-year period.
- Investment of accumulated lump-sum assets in fixed-income securities (such as certificates of deposit, government bonds, municipal bonds, etc.) will yield an inflation-adjusted annual income one-half its initial value at the end of a 15-year period.

A long-term-growth investment program is also essential for accumulating sufficient assets to finance a good college educa-

TABLE 2
WHAT IS A LONG-TERM-GROWTH INVESTMENT PROGRAM?

A LONG-TERM-GROWTH INVESTMENT PROGRAM INCREASES THE VALUE (BY A SIGNIFICANT AMOUNT) OF A LUMP-SUM OR PERIODIC INVESTMENT OVER A PERIOD OF FIVE OR MORE YEARS AFTER ADJUSTMENT FOR:

- ☐ INFLATION ONLY (FOR TAX-QUALIFIED INVESTMENT PROGRAMS; E.G. IRAs)
- ☐ INFLATION AND INCOME TAXES (FOR TAXABLE INVESTMENT PROGRAMS)

NOTE: IN ORDER TO INCREASE THE VALUE OF AN INVESTMENT AFTER ADJUSTMENT FOR INFLATION AND INCOME TAXES, THE ANNUAL GROSS RETURN MUST BE GREATER THAN 7.1%. THIS FIGURE ASSUMES THAT:

- THE LONG TERM INFLATION RATE IS 5.0%
- THE FEDERAL/STATE INCOME TAX RATE IS 30%

TABLE 3
WHY IS A LONG-TERM-GROWTH INVESTMENT PROGRAM ESSENTIAL?

1. TO ACHIEVE A COMFORTABLE RETIREMENT CONSIDERING THAT:

   - ☐ SOCIAL SECURITY INCOME PROVIDES FOR A STANDARD OF LIVING JUST ABOVE THE POVERTY LINE.
   - ☐ MOST COMPANY PENSIONS DO NOT PROVIDE FOR INFLATION (OR COST-OF-LIVING) ADJUSTMENTS. INFLATION WILL REDUCE THE VALUE OF PENSION INCOME BY 50% AFTER 15 YEARS.
   - ☐ INVESTMENT OF ACCUMULATED LUMP-SUM ASSETS IN FIXED-INCOME SECURITIES (MONEY MARKET FUNDS, CDS, ETC.) WILL YIELD INCOME THAT IS ERODED ANNUALLY BY INFLATION AND INCOME TAXES.

2. TO PROVIDE FOR THE COLLEGE EDUCATION OF CHILDREN AND GRAND-CHILDREN AT A TIME WHEN TUITION FEES ARE INCREASING AT A RATE CONSIDERABLY GREATER THAN THE INFLATION RATE.

tion for children or grandchildren over a period of four or more years per child. Such an investment program must cope with the fact that annual college costs have been increasing at rates much greater than annual inflation rates.

Implementing a Long-Term-Growth Investment Program

There are several widely used approaches to implementing an individual's long-term-growth investment program as indicated below. [See Table 4] One could use a broker, money manager, financial planner, or an investment advisor. An individual might join an investment club such as one supported by the National Association of Investment Clubs (NAIC). Certain individuals might prefer to do-it-themselves.

■ Why not invest through a financial services professional?

The majority of American investors employ a financial services professional (i.e., a broker, a money manager or a newsletter publisher) for managing their long-term investment program. Such a choice may be a good one if you have selected one of the better performing investment managers.

How do you know when you have a "better performing" investment manager? A commonly used standard of stock market investment performance is the return achieved by the Standard & Poor's (S&P) 500 Index. During the 11-year period from 1982 to 1992, this index had a mean annualized return (MAR) of 16.7%. *Mean annualized return* (MAR) is the same as compounded rate of return. *See Appendix A if you are not familiar with any of the terms that are used.* An individual investor could have achieved approximately this return by investing in an S&P 500 index mutual fund; i.e., a mutual fund that invests in the 500 stocks that comprise the S&P 500 Index. Figure 1 shows that an average of 59% of the US. professional money managers did **not** outperform the S&P 500 Index during the 10-year period from 1982 to 1991.

If you select one of the 41% of professional money managers who outperformed the S&P 500 Index, you would have achieved a mean annualized return of approximately 15% (or more) after adjustment for management fees.

■ Why not form an investment club?

An investment club consists of a group of individuals who contribute monthly payments into a group investment fund. The club members work together to select stocks and/or mutual funds for investment of the group's assets. The National Asso-

TABLE 4
ALTERNATE APPROACHES FOR
IMPLEMENTING A LONG-TERM-GROWTH INVESTMENT PROGRAM

1. VIA A FINANCIAL SERVICES PROFESSIONAL SUCH AS:

   ☐ BROKER
   ☐ MONEY MANAGER
   ☐ FINANCIAL PLANNER
   ☐ INVESTMENT ADVISER

2. VIA AN INVESTMENT CLUB SUPPORTED BY THE NATIONAL ASSOCIATION OF INVESTMENT CLUBS (NAIC)

3. DO-IT-YOURSELF (SEE TABLE 5)

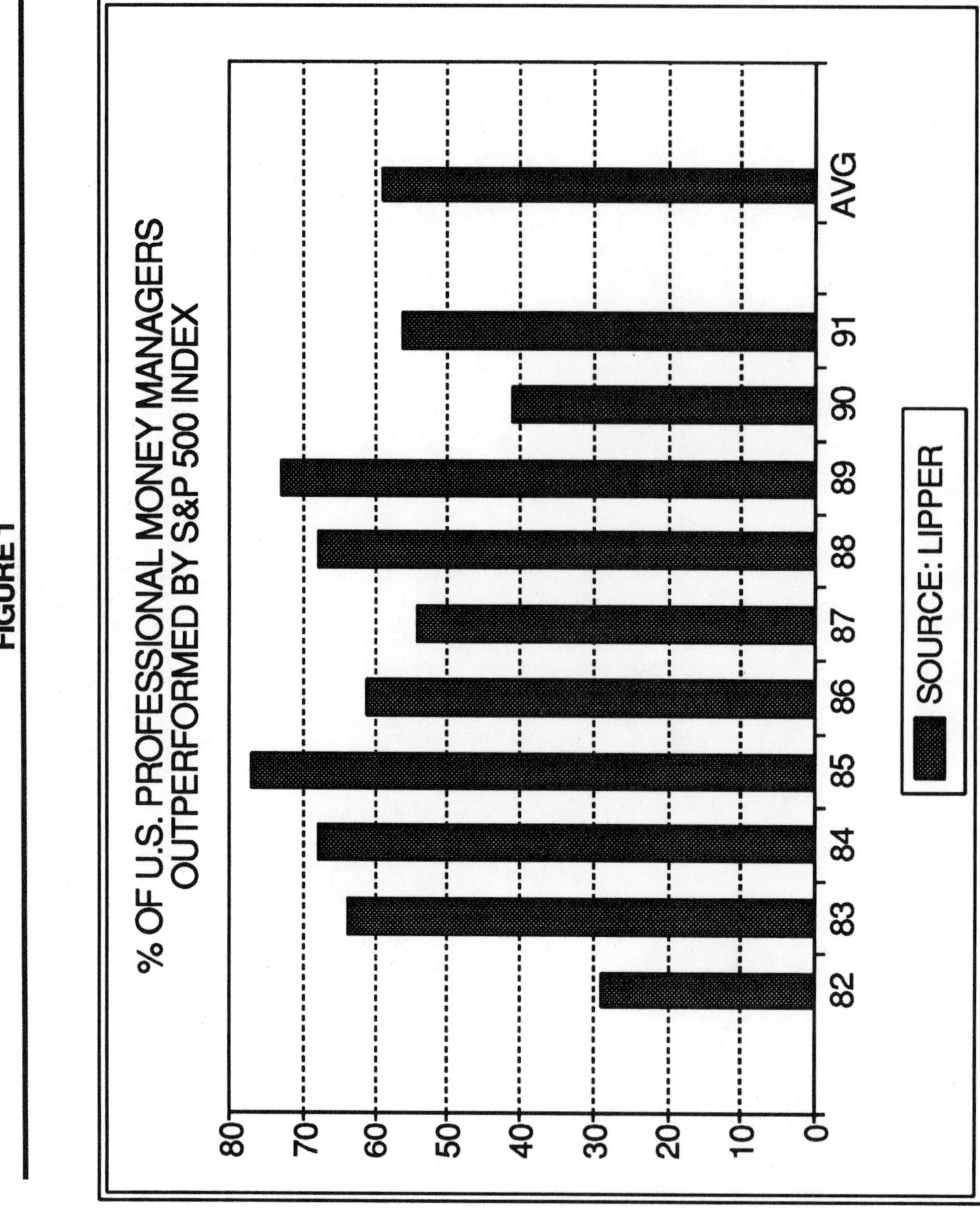
FIGURE 1
% OF U.S. PROFESSIONAL MONEY MANAGERS
OUTPERFORMED BY S&P 500 INDEX
80
70
60
50
40
30
20
10
0
82
83
84
85
86
87
88
89
90
91
AVG
SOURCE: LIPPER

ciation of Investment Corporation (NAIC) provides comprehensive information regarding club organization and investment methodology. This approach requires dedicated time and effort but less than the do-it-yourself approach described later in the book. Table 5 lists the investment information sources used by investment clubs.

■ Why not become a do-it-yourself investment manager?

Available to any American investor is a glut of financial information in newspapers, magazines, newsletters and books (see Table 5). Selecting the top-performing stocks or mutual funds requires a substantial amount of time and the ability to absorb and to synthesize the large amount of information available. It may be difficult to devote so much time and effort if you are working full time and have a family to support. Yet, the best time to initiate a long-term-growth investment program occurs in your thirties and forties when you may be strapped for time. Recognition of this problem has led to the establishment of two types of organizations: (1) newsletters that evaluate the past performance of various investment vehicles and (2) nonprofit investment educational organizations. These are discussed below.

Investment Performance Evaluators

During the past 12 years, at least two newsletters have been established to evaluate objectively, the past performance of several investment vehicles. These two newsletters are the *Hulbert Financial Digest* and the *MoniResearch Newsletter.*

Established in 1980, the *Hulbert Financial Digest* publishes the annual returns that would have been achieved by following the advice of over 150 stock and mutual fund newsletters. In addition, the newsletter periodically selects the top-performing newsletters over specified time periods. The Hulbert Financial Digest, Inc. is located at 316 Commerce Street, Alexandria, VA 22314 (703-683-5905).

Established in 1985, the *MoniResearch Newsletter* evaluates the past performance of professional money managers who employ market timing to switch assets from stocks or stock mutual funds to money market funds or vice versa.

This newsletter considers only those money managers who will provide a continuous record of customer statements for the period under study. This data is used by *MoniResearch* to validate the historic Buy/Sell signals claimed by a money manager. The newsletter computes the annualized rates of return (for one,

TABLE 5
DO-IT-YOURSELF INVESTMENT INFORMATION SOURCES

1. DAILY NEWSPAPERS SUCH AS:
   - ☐ WALL STREET JOURNAL
   - ☐ NEW YORK TIMES
   - ☐ INVESTORS DAILY

2. MAGAZINES AND PERIODICALS SUCH AS:
   - ☐ FORBES
   - ☐ BARRON'S
   - ☐ MONEY

3. INVESTMENT NEWSLETTERS SUCH AS:

   3.1 PERFORMANCE EVALUATORS SUCH AS:

   - ☐ HULBERT FINANCIAL DIGEST
   - ☐ MONIRESEARCH NEWSLETTER

   3.2 NEWSLETTERS (PROVIDING SPECIFIC BUY/SELL RECOMMENDATIONS SUCH AS:

   - ☐ SYSTEMS & FORECASTS
   - ☐ INVESTORS INTELLIGENCE
   - ☐ GROWTH FUND GUIDE
   - ☐ GRANVILLE MARKET LTR.

4. INVESTMENT EDUCATIONAL ORGANIZATIONS SUCH AS:

   - ☐ AMERICAN ASSOCIATION OF INDIVIDUAL INVESTORS (AAII)
   - ☐ ASSOCIATION OF MUTUAL FUND INVESTORS (AMFI)

three and five years) for the S&P 500 Index when timed by these signals. Over 40 professional money managers are evaluated in this manner. The *MoniResearch Newsletter* is located at P.O. Box 19146, Portland, OR 97219 (503-625-6716)

Investment Educational Organizations

In 1978, James Cloonan founded the American Association of Individual Investors (AAII) as an independent, nonprofit corporation. Its objective is to educate individuals regarding a wide range of investment vehicles. To achieve this objective, AAII publishes a monthly journal and conducts investment seminars throughout the country. In addition, AAII has established over 40 chapters in the major metropolitan areas. These chapters hold six or more meetings per year at which invited speakers make presentations on a wide range of investment topics.

In 1986, the authors organized a Mutual Funds Special Interest Group (MFG) under the AAII Philadelphia chapter. The objective of this group was to educate individuals regarding only one investment vehicle; namely, mutual funds. To achieve this objective, MFG conducted investment research and evaluated the performance of a large number of mutual fund investment systems. Such evaluation was performed in the same manner as described above for the *Hulbert Financial Digest* and the *MoniResearch Newsletter.* The results of the MFG research were published in bimonthly meeting notes or a newsletter and mailed to MFG members before bimonthly group meetings. At these meetings, slides of the tables and charts in the MFG newsletter were presented to explain the contents and to stimulate discussion.

In September 1992, the MFG members and Board of Directors voted to establish the Association of Mutual Fund Investors (AMFI), an *independent,* nonprofit corporation. AMFI provides the same mutual fund educational services as previously provided by MFG.

Table 6 summarizes the comparative characteristics of AAII and AMFI. Table 7 is a copy of the Table of Contents of the 1993 issue of the AMFI January/February meeting notes.

TABLE 6
INVESTMENT EDUCATIONAL ORGANIZATIONS
COMPARATIVE CHARACTERISTICS

CHARACTERISTIC	AMERICAN ASSOCIATION OF INDIVIDUAL INVESTORS (AAII)	ASSOCIATION OF MUTUAL FUND INVESTORS (AMFI)
ORGANIZATION TYPE	INDEPENDENT, NOT-FOR-PROFIT CORPORATION	INDEPENDENT, NOT-FOR-PROFIT CORPORATION
STATED OBJECTIVE	ASSIST INDIVIDUALS IN BECOMING EFFECTIVE MANAGERS OF THEIR ASSETS THROUGH PROGRAMS OF EDUCATION, INFORMATION AND RESEARCH.	ASSIST INDIVIDUALS IN BECOMING EFFECTIVE MANAGERS OF THEIR **MUTUAL FUND** INVESTMENTS BY CONDUCTING PROGRAMS OF INVESTMENT RESEARCH, EDUCATION AND INFORMATION DISSEMINATION.
PRIMARY PUBLICATION	MONTHLY JOURNAL COVERING A WIDE RANGE OF INVESTMENT TOPICS SUCH AS FINANCIAL PLANNING, TECHNICAL ANALYSIS, STOCK SELECTION, MUTUAL FUNDS, ETC.	BIMONTHLY JOURNAL THAT PRESENTS THE RESULTS OF MUTUAL FUND INVESTMENT RESEARCH. RESEARCH TOPICS INCLUDE (1) MARKET TIMING MODELS; (2) GROWTH FUND SELECTION METHODOLOGIES; AND (3) PERFORMANCE EVALUATION OF MUTUAL FUND INVESTMENT SYSTEMS (SEE TABLE 7).
LOCAL CHAPTER MEETINGS	INVITED SPEAKERS MAKE PRESENTATIONS ON A WIDE RANGE OF INVESTMENT TOPICS	RESEARCHERS PRESENT SLIDES OF THE TABLES/CHARTS IN THE BIMONTHLY JOURNAL TO EXPLAIN AND TO STIMULATE DISCUSSION OF THE RESEARCH TOPICS.

TABLE 7
ASSOCIATION OF MUTUAL FUND INVESTORS (AMFI):
PHILADELPHIA CHAPTER AMFI MEETING NOTES

ISSUE 93-1 | **CONTENTS** | **JANUARY/FEBRUARY 1993**

2: INVESTMENT FUNDAMENTALS

INTRODUCTION

This chapter provides background information regarding various investment vehicles with emphasis upon mutual funds. In addition, we will show why growth mutual funds offer long-term investors many advantages including superior long-term returns as compared with money market securities, CDs and government bonds. Finally, we will introduce several criteria for evaluating the past performance of mutual fund investment systems as a prelude to selecting a system for investment.

Major Investment Vehicles

Tables 7 and 8 list six major types of investment vehicles with subordinate categories shown under debt securities and under mutual funds. These six investment vehicles are:

- Real Estate
- Debt Securities (Bills and Bonds)
- Equity Securities (Common Stock)
- Leveraged Investments (warrants, stock rights, options and futures)
- Collectibles (art, antiques, stamps, etc.)
- Mutual Funds

REAL ESTATE offers an investor the opportunity to invest in a tangible asset. There are two basic types of real estate investment: (1) direct investment in undeveloped land, residential rental property and commercial property and (2) indirect investment in pooled real estate investment arrangements such as real estate investment trusts (REITs), limited partnerships and mortgage-backed investments, e.g., *Ginnie Maes.*

DEBT SECURITIES represent a loan from the investor to a company or government. Debt securities are usually fixed-income securities that generally stress current fixed income and offer little or no opportunity for appreciation in value. Such appreciation is known as capital gains. They are usually liquid and carry less market risk than other types of investments. As inter-

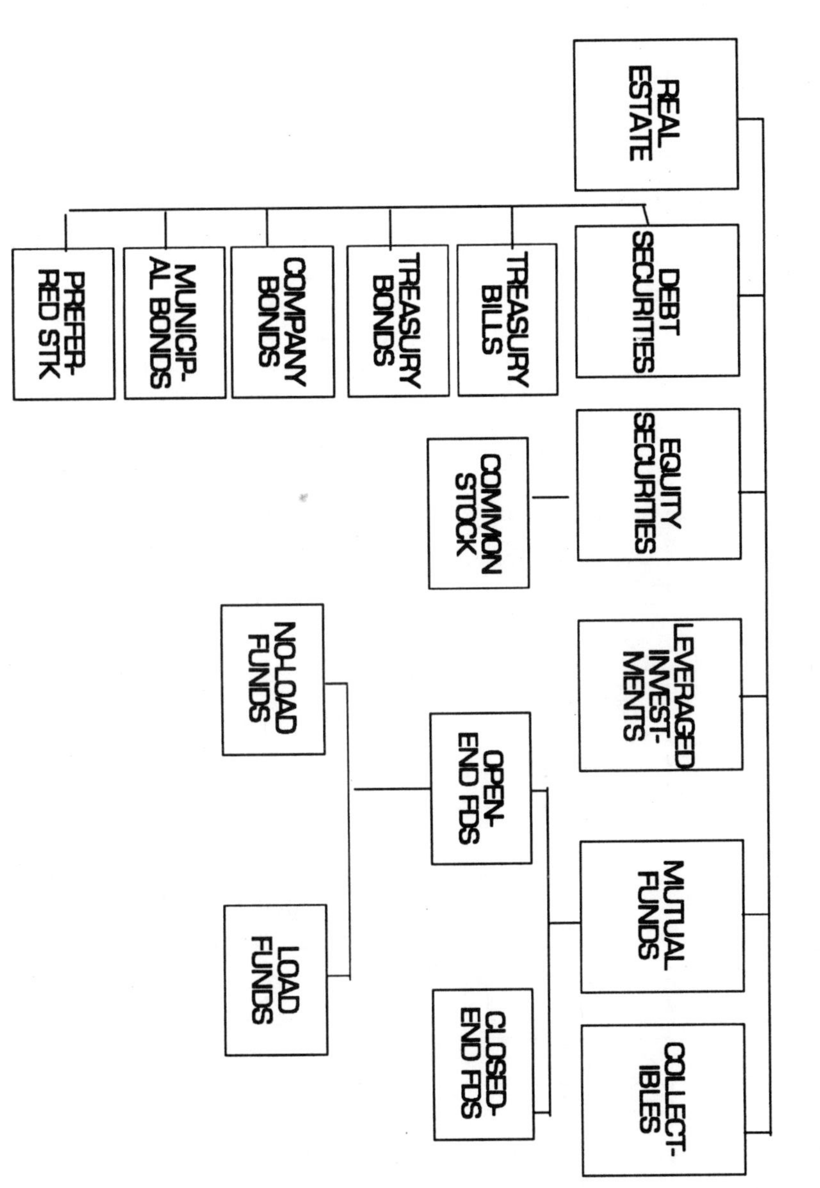

TABLE 8
MAJOR INVESTMENT VEHICLES

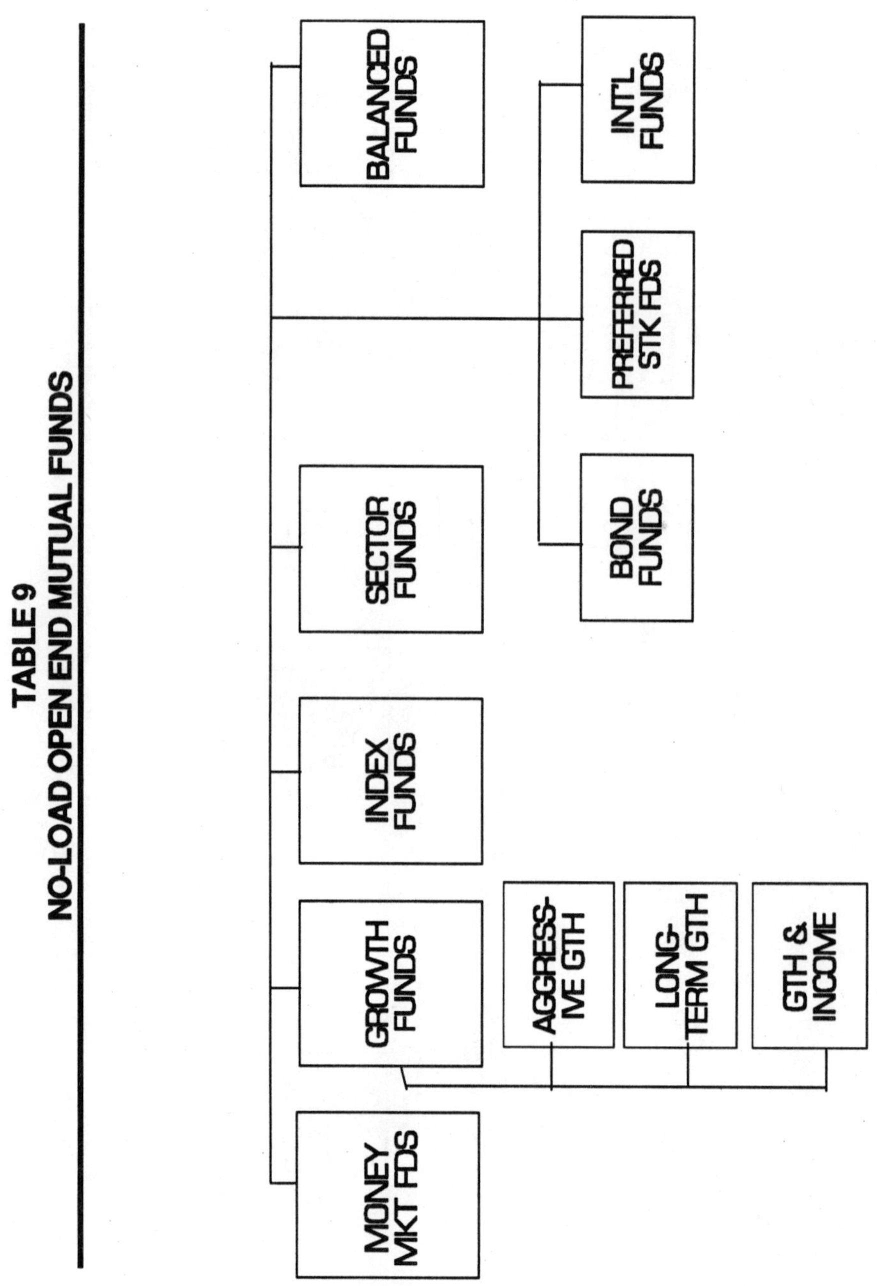
TABLE 9
NO-LOAD OPEN END MUTUAL FUNDS
MONEY MKT FDS
GROWTH FUNDS
INDEX FUNDS
SECTOR FUNDS
BALANCED FUNDS
AGGRESS-IVE GTH
LONG-TERM GTH
GTH & INCOME
BOND FUNDS
PREFERRED STK FDS
INT'L FUNDS

est rates drop, the price of fixed-income investments increases and vice versa. Table 10A lists and briefly describes five types of debt securities.

EQUITY SECURITIES (common stocks) represent ownership in a corporation. These securities provide the potential (not a guarantee) for both current income (as periodic dividends) and future capital gains (or losses). They are usually liquid when traded through a major stock exchange and may bear greater short-term risk (or volatility) than fixed-income investments. (See Table 10B).

LEVERAGED INVESTMENTS are investment vehicles in which an investor can participate with a small sum of money. Such investments include warrants, stock rights, options and futures. The value of these investments is derived from the value of their underlying securities. Options convey the right to purchase a security at a specified price, for a stated period of time. You may want to acquire an option to take advantage of an expected rise in the price of an underlying stock. Option prices are directly related to the prices of the common stock to which they apply. The types of options include stock rights, warrants and calls and puts. Investing in options is considered to be very risky and requires specialized knowledge.

Futures are contracts to purchase or sell a given amount of an item for a given price in the future. Items that trade in futures include commodities and financial instruments. Commodity contracts are guarantees by a seller to deliver a commodity such as cotton or cocoa. Financial contracts are commitments by a seller to deliver a financial instrument, such as a Treasury bill or a specific amount of a foreign currency. Futures can be risky. You need specialized knowledge and skill to invest profitably in futures.

COLLECTIBLES are tangible assets such as precious gems, art, antiques, stamps, Chinese ceramics and rare books. Tangibles can be inflation hedges. In the 1970s, oil, gold, US coins, silver and stamps all had the highest compounded rates of return (above 20%). However, from 1980 to 1985, financial assets such as bonds, stocks and Treasury bills had higher returns than every category of tangible assets. Investing in collectibles can yield high profits for investors with specialized product and market knowledge.

TABLE 10A
TYPES OF DEBT SECURITIES

1. TREASURY BILLS (T-BILLS)
   - ☐ SHORT-TERM GOVERNMENT SECURITIES MATURING IN 3/6/12 MONTHS
   - ☐ TRADED IN UNITS OF $10,000
   - ☐ EXTREMELY LIQUID
   - ☐ EXTREMELY LOW DOLLAR RISK (BACKED BY U.S. GOVERNMENT)

2. CERTIFICATES OF DEPOSIT (CDS)
   - ☐ SECURITY REPRESENTS LOAN TO A COMMERCIAL BANK OR THRIFT INSTITUTION
   - ☐ FIXED TERM FROM THREE MONTHS TO TEN YEARS
   - ☐ PROVIDES ANNUAL FIXED INCOME
   - ☐ INSURED BY FEDERAL GOVERNEMNT UP TO $100,000 PER ACCOUNT PER INSTITUTION

3. TREASURY & CORPORATE BONDS
   - ☐ SECURITY REPRESENTS LONG-TERM LOAN TO U.S. TREASURY OR A CORPORATION
   - ☐ PROVIDES ANNUAL FIXED INCOME BUT LITTLE OR NO CAPITAL APPRECIATION IF BOUGHT AND HELD
   - ☐ REPAYS PRINCIPAL AT END OF TERM
   - ☐ MANY TYPES OF BONDS; E.G. INCOME, MORTGAGE, DEBENTURE, ETC.

4. MUNICIPAL BONDS ARE SIMILAR TO TREASURY BONDS, EXCEPT
   - ☐ LOAN IS MADE TO A MUNICIPALITY
   - ☐ INTEREST INCOME IS NOT SUBJECT TO FEDERAL INCOME TAXES NOR STATE/LOCAL INCOME TAXES UNDER CERTAIN CONDITIONS

5. PREFERRED STOCK
   - ☐ SECURITY REPRESENTS A SHARE OF OWNERSHIP IN A CORPORATION
   - ☐ SHAREHOLDERS EXERCISE CONTROL OF CORPORATION BY ELECTING DIRECTORS
   - ☐ PROVIDES A FIXED DIVIDEND BUT NO CAPITAL APPRECIATION

TABLE 10B
TYPES OF EQUITY SECURITIES

COMMON STOCKS

- ☐ SECURITY REPRESENTS A SHARE OF OWNERSHIP IN A CORPORATION
- ☐ SHAREHOLDERS EXERCISE CONTROL OF CORPORATION BY ELECTING DIRECTORS
- ☐ PROVIDE POTENTIAL FOR INCOME AND CAPITAL GAINS
- ☐ MANY TYPES OF COMMON STOCKS; E.G. BLUE CHIP, GROWTH, INCOME, CYCLICAL, DEFENSIVE AND SPECULATIVE

A MUTUAL FUND is an investment company run by professional managers who pool the money of many individual investors to purchase a diverse portfolio of securities. Participation is characterized by ownership of fund shares. Each share or unit of ownership represents a pro-rata interest in each of the fund's investments. Table 8 uses a flow chart to illustrate the various categories and types of mutual funds.

Mutual Fund Advantages

There are six major advantages of investing in mutual funds:

- DIVERSIFICATION. Each fund share gives you pro-rata ownership of a cross section of stocks, bonds or other investments. Such diversification reduces risk as compared with holding a few individual securities.
- LIQUIDITY. You can redeem the shares owned within a few days by a telephone call or letter.
- AUTOMATIC REINVESTMENT OF DISTRIBUTIONS. Most funds will automatically reinvest dividend and capital gains distributions.
- SWITCHING. Assets can be transferred (usually by telephone) from one mutual fund to another to accommodate changes in the investment climate.
- SMALL MINIMUM INVESTMENT. You can achieve diversification with a small investment ($250 to $1,000).
- AUTOMATIC WITHDRAWALS. You can withdraw money from most funds on a regular basis.

Types of Mutual Funds

As indicated in Table 9 and Table 11A, there are two basic types of mutual funds; namely, open-end and closed-end funds.

In **open-end funds,** you buy and sell shares from and to the fund. This type of fund offers to sell and redeem shares on a continual basis for an indefinite time period. Shares are purchased at the ***net asset value*** (NAV) plus commission (if any). The NAV is equal to the fund's net worth (assets minus liabilities) divided by the number of outstanding shares. The number of outstanding shares is constantly changing as investors buy and redeem shares. The NAV of these funds is listed daily in all major newspapers.

Closed-end funds operate with a fixed number of shares. The shares of these funds are traded among individuals in a secon-

TABLE 11A
TYPES OF MUTUAL FUNDS

1. A MUTUAL FUND IS AN INVESTMENT COMPANY THAT:
   - ☐ IS SUBJECT TO THE INVESTMENT COMPANY ACT OF 1940
   - ☐ IS RUN BY PROFESSIONAL INVESTMENT MANAGERS
   - ☐ POOLS THE ASSETS OF MANY INDIVIDUAL INVESTORS
   - ☐ BUYS A DIVERSE PORTFOLIO OF MANY INDIVIDUAL SECURITIES

2. BASIC TYPES OF MUTUAL FUNDS
   - ☐ OPEN-END FUNDS
   - ☐ CLOSED-END FUNDS

3. OPEN-END MUTUAL FUNDS
   - ☐ INVESTOR INVESTS BY BUYING SHARES FROM THE COMPANY AND REDEEMS INVESTMENT BY SELLING SHARES BACK TO THE COMPANY
   - ☐ COMPANY CONTINUOUSLY OFFERS TO BUY AND SELL SHARES FROM AND TO INDIVIDUAL INVESTORS
   - ☐ INVESTOR PURCHASES SHARES FROM THE COMPANY AT NET ASSET VALUE PLUS COMMISSION (IF ANY)
   - ☐ COMPANY REDEEMS SHARES AT NET ASSET VALUE LESS A REDEMPTION FEE (IF ANY)

4. CLOSED-END MUTUAL FUNDS
   - ☐ COMPANY HAS A FIXED NUMBER OF SHARES
   - ☐ INVESTOR INVESTS BY BUYING SHARES (IN A STOCK MARKET) FROM OTHER INDIVIDUALS AND REDEEMS INVESTMENT BY SELLING SHARES (IN A STOCK MARKET) TO OTHER INDIVIDUALS
   - ☐ SHARE PRICE MAY BE MORE OR LESS THAN NET ASSET VALUE

dary market in the same manner as common stocks. The share price of a closed-end fund may differ from its NAV by a discount or a premium.

As is shown in Table 9, open-end funds may be further subdivided into load funds and no-load funds. **Load funds** are mutual funds that charge a sales commission (called a load) when fund shares are purchased **and/or** charge a redemption (or exit) fee when fund shares are redeemed. Typically, the load or sales commission varies from 2% to 8.5% of the investment. The redemption fee varies from a flat $5 to 2% of the amount redeemed. Another type of an exit fee is the deferred sales charge or back-end load. These charges vary with the duration of the investment and are eliminated after a predetermined time. **No-load funds** do not charge a load or sales commission nor any type of exit or redemption fee. *In this book, we are concerned with mutual fund investment systems consisting only of open-end, no-load funds.*

Types of Open-End Mutual Funds

As indicated in Table 9 and Table 11B, there are at least eight types of open-end mutual funds, as follows:

- **Money Market Funds.** These mutual funds invest exclusively in debt securities maturing in less than one year, such as government securities, commercial paper and certificates of deposit. These funds provide no risk of loss of the principal amount because the share price never changes. They are known as dollar funds because the share price is always $1. However, the interest income fluctuates in the same manner as the 3-month Treasury bills.
- **Growth Funds.** These mutual funds invest primarily in common stocks. Their objective is to achieve capital growth. There are three basic types that strive for: (1) maximum capital appreciation; (2) long-term growth with income secondary; or (3) both current income and capital appreciation. The share price of these funds fluctuates; therefore, these funds are considered as having greater short-term risk than money market and bond funds.
- **Index Funds.** These funds invest in a portfolio of common stocks that are determined by a major market index such as the Standard and Poor's 500 (S&P 500) Index. This index consists of the 500 largest-capitalization stocks listed on the New York Stock Exchange. The index is a market-value index; i.e., the

TABLE 11B
TYPES OF OPEN-END MUTUAL FUNDS

1. **MONEY MARKET FUNDS** INVEST EXCLUSIVELY IN DEBT SECURITIES THAT MATURE IN LESS THAN 12 MONTHS
   - ☐ FIXED PRICE PER SHARE
   - ☐ DIVIDENDS ARE SLIGHTLY GREATER THAN 3-MONTH T-BILL RATE

2. **GROWTH FUNDS** INVEST PRIMARILY IN COMMON STOCKS
   - ☐ PRICE PER SHARE FLUCTUATES
   - ☐ PROVIDES POTENTIAL FOR DIVIDEND INCOME AND CAPITAL GAINS
   - ☐ TYPES INCLUDE:
     - A. AGGRESSIVE GROWTH
     - B. LONG-TERM GROWTH
     - C. GROWTH AND INCOME

3. **INDEX FUNDS** INVEST IN A PORTFOLIO OF COMMON STOCKS THAT ARE INCLUDED IN A MAJOR STOCK MARKET INDEX SUCH AS:
   - ☐ STANDARD & POOR'S 500 INDEX (S&P 500 INDEX)
   - ☐ DOW JONES INDUSTRIAL AVERAGE (DJIA)

4. **BALANCED FUNDS** INVEST IN BOTH COMMON STOCKS AND BONDS

5. **SECTOR FUNDS** INVEST IN A PORTFOLIO OF COMMON STOCKS COVERING ONE OR TWO FIELDS OR INDUSTRIES; E.G. HEALTH SCIENCE, LEISURE, TECHNOLOGY, ENVIRONMENTAL SERVICES, ETC.

6. **OTHER FUNDS** SUCH AS BOND, PREFERRED STOCK AND INTERNATIONAL FUNDS

stocks are weighted by their market value each day. The S&P 500 Index is designed to portray the pattern of common stock price movement. It is used by many investors as a yardstick to help evaluate the performance of mutual funds and mutual fund investment systems.

- **Balanced Funds.** These funds invest in both common stocks and bonds and often in preferred stock. Their objective is to provide income and some capital appreciation.
- **Sector Funds.** These funds invest in a portfolio of common stocks covering one or two industries such as automotive, utilities, transportation, etc. Consequently, these funds are considered as having greater risk than growth funds because of their higher volatility.
- **Bonds and Preferred Stocks.** These funds invest in bonds and preferred stock with emphasis on income rather than growth. There are two types of bond funds; namely, funds that invest in (1) corporate bonds or (2) tax-free municipal bonds.
- **International Funds.** These funds invest in the stocks and bonds of corporations traded on foreign exchanges.

Why Growth Mutual Funds?

As previously indicated, our objective is to select mutual fund investment systems that achieve substantial long-term growth of invested assets after adjustment for inflation and income taxes. Growth mutual funds offer the best vehicle for achieving this primary objective. Table 12 lists five advantages of investing in growth funds. Except for the first, all of these advantages are the same as those previously described for all mutual funds. We will show that common stocks (or growth mutual funds) have had superior long-term returns as compared with other investment vehicles such as money market funds, certificates of deposit (CDs) and bonds. In addition, we demonstrate that the risk of common stock investment decreases substantially as the investment holding period increases beyond five years.

Superior Long-Term Returns

Figures 2A, 2B and 2C and Tables 13 compare the average annual returns of three investment vehicles (money market funds, government bonds and common stocks represented by the S&P 500 Index) during the 20-year period from 1972 through 1991. This period includes the 1973-74 severe bear market, the 1987 crash and many market corrections. Four time periods are indi-

TABLE 12
WHY GROWTH (COMMON STOCK) MUTUAL FUNDS?

1. **SUPERIOR LONG-TERM RETURNS.** COMMON STOCKS HAVE CONSISTENTLY OUTPERFORMED OTHER INVESTMENT VEHICLES SUCH AS MONEY MARKET FUNDS, CDS AND BONDS.

2. **DIVERSIFICATION.** EACH FUND SHARE PROVIDES A CROSS-SECTION OF COMMON STOCK INVESTMENTS THEREBY SUBSTANTIALLY REDUCING RISK WITHOUT REQUIRING A LARGE INVESTMENT.

3. **LIQUIDITY.** YOU CAN REDEEM SHARES IN MOST FUNDS WITHIN ONE DAY BY TELEPHONE.

4. **SWITCHING FROM ONE FUND TO ANOTHER.** WHEN MARKET CONDITIONS CHANGE, YOU CAN SWITCH ASSETS FROM ONE FUND TO (1) ANOTHER FUND IN THE SAME FAMILY OF FUNDS AT NO FEE OR (2) ANOTHER FUND IN A DIFFERENT FAMILY FOR A SMALL FEE.

5. **AUTOMATIC REINVESTMENT OF FUND DISTRIBUTIONS.** WHEN A FUND DISTRIBUTES DIVIDEND INCOME AND/OR CAPITAL GAINS, THESE DISTRIBUTIONS ARE USED TO PURCHASE ADDITIONAL FUND SHARES.

FIGURE 2A

AVERAGE ANNUAL RETURNS (1972 TO 1991)
MONEY MKT FDS VS BONDS VS STOCKS
AVERAGE ANNUAL RETURN (%)
20
18
16
14
12
10
8
6
4
2
0
87-91
82-91
77-91
72-91
MONEY MKT FDS
GOVT BONDS
S&P 500 INDEX

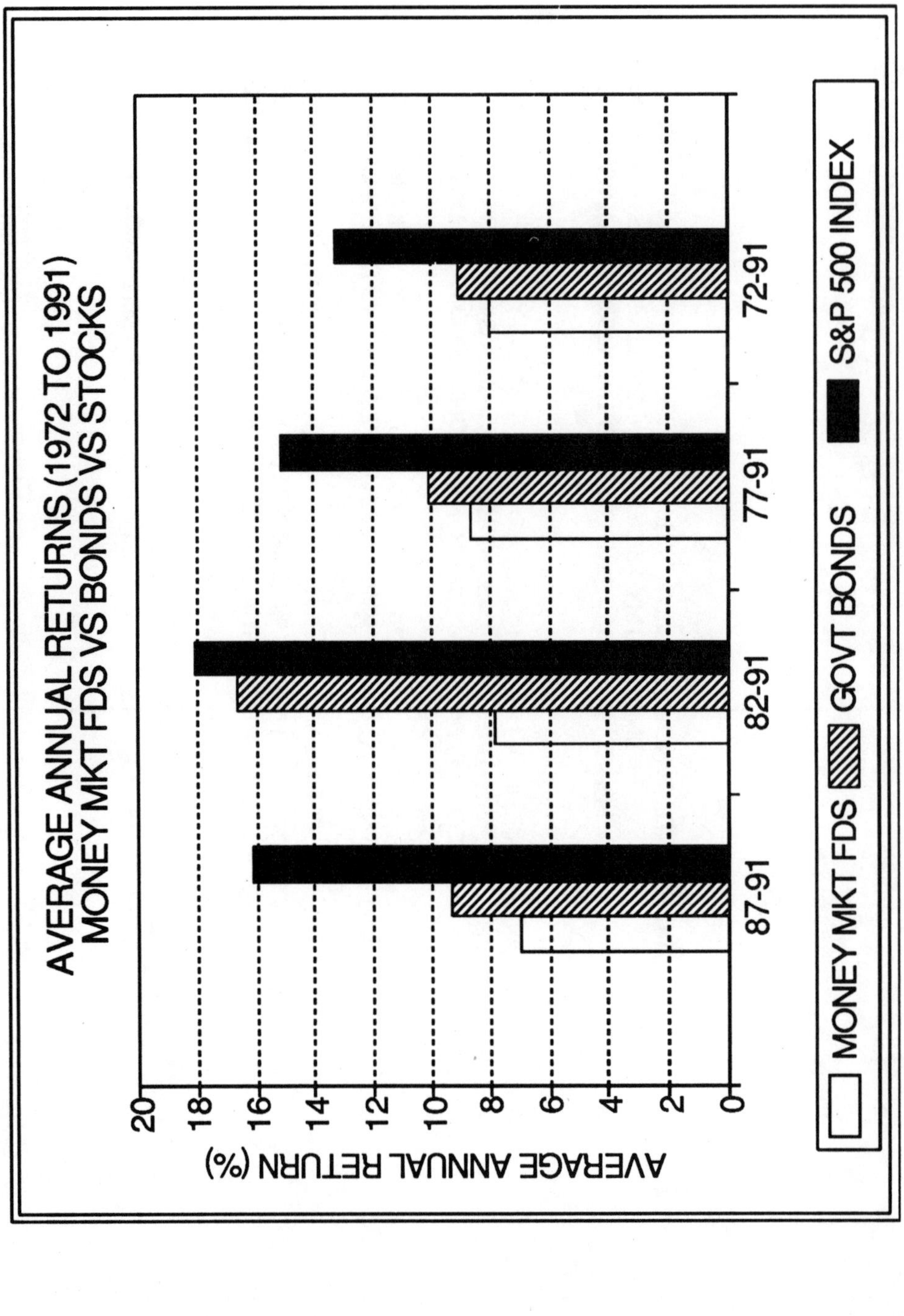

FIGURE 2B

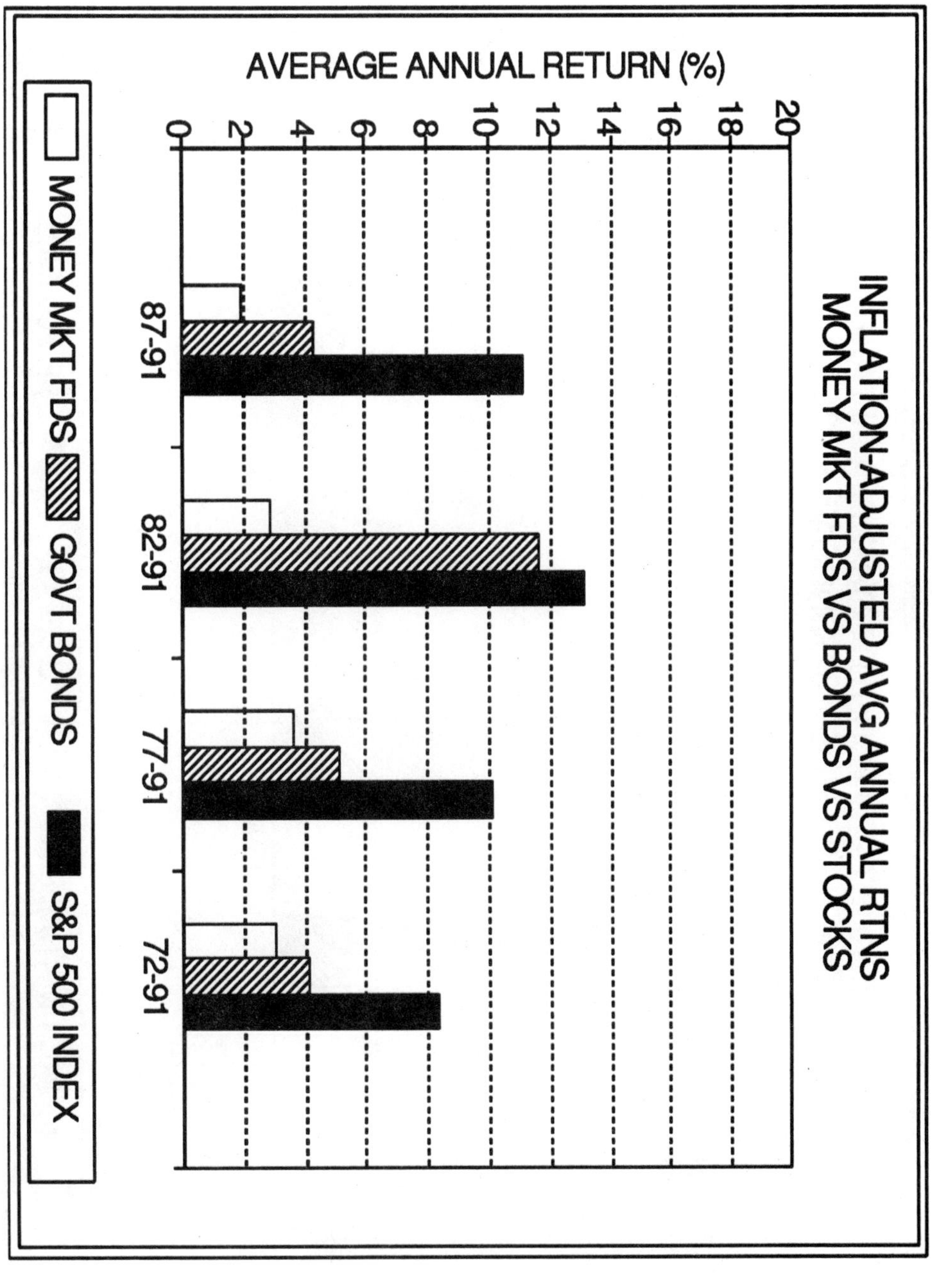

INFLATION-ADJUSTED AVG ANNUAL RTNS
MONEY MKT FDS VS BONDS VS STOCKS
AVERAGE ANNUAL RETURN (%)
0
2
4
6
8
10
12
14
16
18
20
87-91
82-91
77-91
72-91
MONEY MKT FDS
GOVT BONDS
S&P 500 INDEX

FIGURE 2C

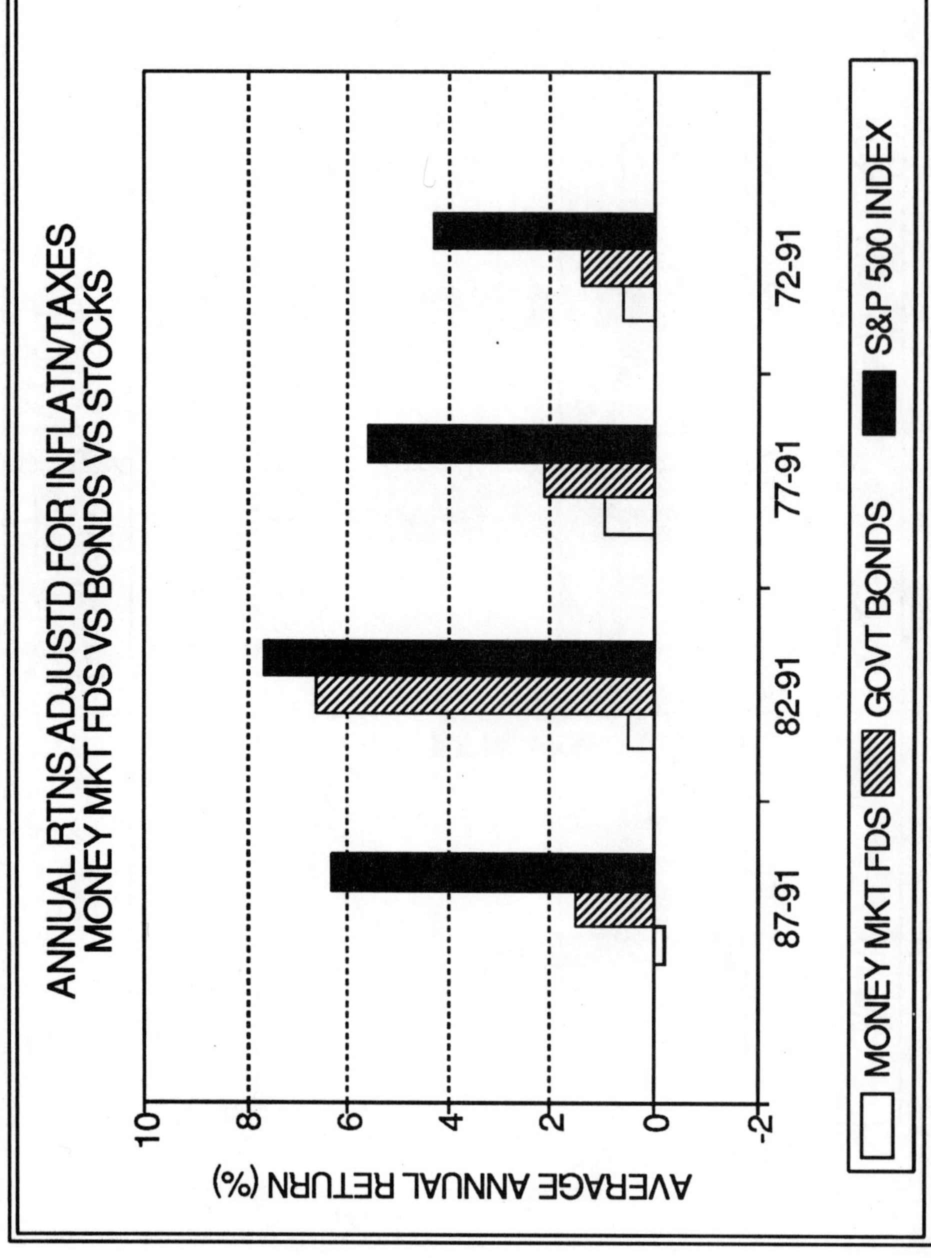
ANNUAL RTNS ADJUSTD FOR INFLATN/TAXES
MONEY MKT FDS VS BONDS VS STOCKS
AVERAGE ANNUAL RETURN (%)
10
8
6
4
2
0
-2
87-91
82-91
77-91
72-91
MONEY MKT FDS
GOVT BONDS
S&P 500 INDEX

TABLE 13
STOCKS HAVE HISTORICALLY REWARDED LONG-TERM INVESTORS
COMPARE THE AVERAGE ANNUAL RETURNS YOU WOULD HAVE RECEIVED

A. GROSS AVERAGE ANNUAL RETURNS (%) (NOTE 1)

IF YOU HAD BOUGHT AND HELD	TIME PERIODS			
	5 YRS (87-91)	10 YRS (82-91)	15 YRS (77-91)	20YRS (72-91)
MONEY MARKET SECURITIES	6.9	7.8	8.6	8.0
LONG-TERM GOVERNMENT BONDS	9.3	16.6	10.1	9.1
STOCKS [S&P 500 INDEX]	16.1	18.1	15.1	13.3
B. AVERAGE ANNUAL RETURNS ADJUSTED FOR 5% ANNUAL INFLATION RATE				
MONEY MARKET SECURITIES	1.9	2.8	3.6	3.0
LONG-TERM GOVERNMENT BONDS	4.3	11.6	5.1	4.1
STOCKS [S&P 500 INDEX]	11.1	13.1	10.1	8.3
C. AVERAGE ANNUAL RETUNS ADJUSTED FOR INFLATION & INCOME TAXES				
MONEY MARKET SECURITIES	-0.2	0.5	1.0	0.6
LONG-TERM GOVERNMENT BONDS	1.5	6.6	2.1	1.4
STOCKS [S&P 500 INDEX]	6.3	7.7	5.6	4.3

NOTE 1. SOURCE: NED DAVIS RESEARCH, ATLANTA, GA.

cated: the 5-year, 10-year, 15-year and 20-year periods ending on December 31, 1991.

Figure 2A and Table 13, part A illustrate the average annual returns *without adjustment for inflation and for income taxes.* This figure and table demonstrate that:

- The S&P 500 Index *outperformed* money market funds and government bonds during all four time periods.
- During the 5-year period (87-91), the S&P Index (with an average return of 16.1%) beat money market funds and government bonds *by significant margins of 9.2% and 6.8%, respectively.*

Figure 2B and Table 13, part b, show the average annual returns *adjusted for a 5% annual inflation rate but without adjustment for annual income taxes.* This would be applicable to investments made in tax-qulaified plans such as IRAs and Keogh plans. The data indicate:

- Again, the S&P 500 *outperformed* money market funds and government bonds during all four time periods.
- During the 5-year period from 1987 to 1991, the Index (with an avaerage annual return of 11.1%) beat money market and government funds *by the same substantial margins of 9.2% and 6.8% respectively.*

Figure 2C and Table 13, part C indicate the average annual returns *adjusted for both inflation and income taxes.* This data is applicable to investments made without benefit of tax-deferred plans. This figure and table indicate that:

- Money market securities provided little or no growth.
- Long-term government bonds provided only 1% to 2% growth except during the 82-91 time period.
- *Common stocks provided 4% to 8% real growth.*

Common Stock Investment Risk

Investment risk is usually equated with investment volatility. The higher the volatility, the greater is the risk. Let us examine the volatility of the S&P 500 Index total return (i.e., including reinvested dividends) during the 32-year period from 1960 to 1991. Table 14A, column 2, indicates the annual return of the index during the 32-year period. The maximum annual return was 37.2% in 1975 and the minimum annual return was -26.5%

TABLE 14A
S&P 500 INDEX MEAN ANNUALIZED RETURNS (MAR) (%) VS. HOLDING PERIOD (YRS)
32-YR PERIOD FROM 1960 TO 1991

	HOLDING PERIOD ENDING AT INDICATED YEAR				
YEAR	**1-YR**	**5-YR**	**10-YR**	**15-YR**	**20-YR**
1960	5.5				
1961	26.9				
1962	-8.7				
1963	22.8				
1964	16.5	11.8			
1965	12.5	13.3			
1966	-10.1	5.7			
1967	24.0	12.4			
1968	11.1	10.2			
1969	-8.4	5.0	8.4		
1970	3.9	3.3	8.2		
1971	14.3	8.4	7.1		
1972	19.0	7.5	9.9		
1973	-14.9	2.0	6.0		
1974	-26.5	-2.4	1.2	4.6	

TABLE 14A CONT'D
S&P 500 INDEX MEAN ANNUALIZED RETURN [MAR] (%)
VS. HOLDING PERIOD [YRS] 32-YEAR PERIOD FROM 1960 TO 1991

	HOLDING PERIOD ENDING AT INDICATED YEAR				
YEAR	**1-YR**	**5-YR**	**10-YR**	**15-YR**	**20-YR**
1975	37.2	3.1	3.2	6.5	
1976	23.9	4.8	6.6	6.3	
1977	-7.1	-0.2	3.6	6.4	
1978	6.6	4.4	3.1	5.4	
1979	18.6	14.8	5.8	5.6	7.1
1980	32.4	14	8.4	6.7	8.3
1981	-5.0	8.1	6.5	7.1	6.8
1982	21.6	14.1	6.7	7.0	8.3
1983	22.5	17.3	10.6	7.7	8.3
1984	6.2	14.8	14.8	8.7	7.8
1985	31.8	14.6	14.3	10.5	8.6
1986	18.8	19.9	13.9	10.8	10.2
1987	5.2	16.5	15.3	9.9	9.3
1988	16.6	15.3	16.3	12.2	9.5
1989	31.7	20.4	17.5	16.6	11.5
1990	-3.1	13.2	13.9	14.0	11.2
1991	30.5	15.4	17.6	14.4	11.9

in 1974. The difference or spread between the maximum and minimum annual returns is one measure of investment volatility. The S&P 500 Index had a spread of 63.7% (37.2 + 26.5) for a holding period of one year. Another measure of risk would be the number of years in which the total return was negative; i.e., a capital loss. The index had eight (8) loss years during the 32-year period; i.e., on the average, there was a loss every fourth year.

Table 14A also shows the mean annualized return (or compounded rate of return) for the S&P 500 Index for holding periods of 5,10,15 and 20 years. Figure 3 and Table 14B illustrate the variation of the spread (between maximum and minimum returns) with the holding period. The figure and table show that the spread decreases from 64% (for a one year holding period) to two (for a five-year holding period) to zero (for holding periods above five).

From the above data, we may conclude that the risk of an investment in a diversified portfolio of common stocks (e.g., S&P 500 Index) or in growth mutual funds decreases substantially as the investment holding period is increased. At holding periods greater than ten years, such risk may be quite acceptable to most long-term investors.

Evaluating Investment System Performance

How does an individual long-term investor select an investment system for his/her use in achieving long-term growth after adjustment for inflation and income taxes? How does such an investor monitor the selected system's performance to determine whether or not the system is performing as expected based upon its past performance? We have developed a set of investment system performance criteria to answer these questions; i.e., to achieve the following objectives:

- Investment System Selection. Select one or more top-performing mutual fund investment systems for subsequent investment.
- Investment System Monitoring. Monitor a selected investment system to determine if and when such system is not performing as expected based upon past performance.

FIGURE 3

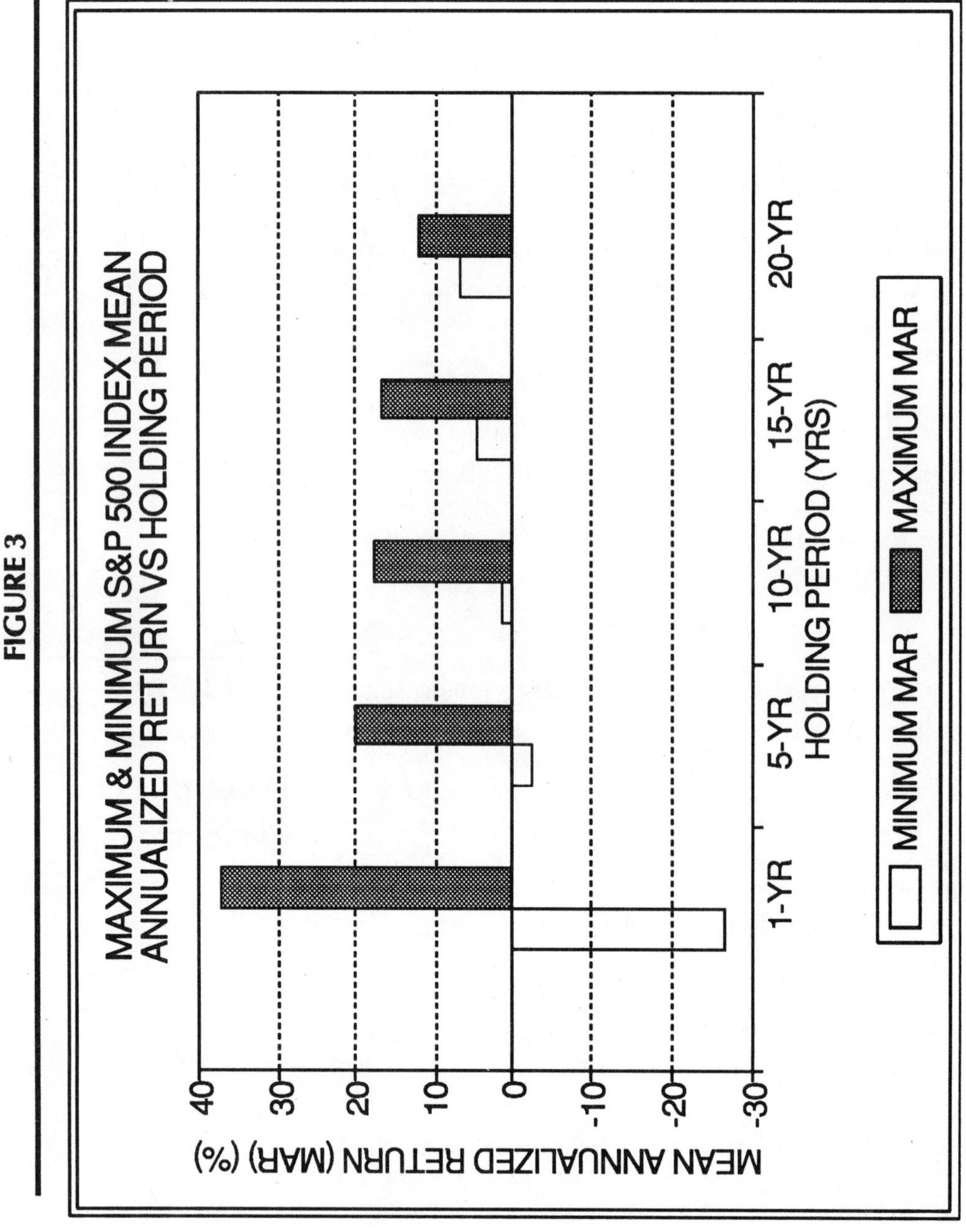
MAXIMUM & MINIMUM S&P 500 INDEX MEAN
ANNUALIZED RETURN VS HOLDING PERIOD
MEAN ANNUALIZED RETURN (MAR) (%)
40
30
20
10
0
-10
-20
-30
1-YR
5-YR
10-YR
15-YR
20-YR
HOLDING PERIOD (YRS)
MINIMUM MAR
MAXIMUM MAR

TABLE 14B
MAXIMUM & MINIMUM S&P 500 MEAN ANNUALIZED RETURNS (MAR) (%)
VS. HOLDING PERIOD (YEARS)
32-YR PERIOD FROM 1960 TO 1991

	HOLDING PERIOD				
	1-YR	**5-YR**	**10-YR**	**15-YR**	**20-YR**
MINIMUM MAR	-26.5	-2.4	1.2	4.6	6.8
MAXIMUM MAR	37.2	20.4	17.6	16.6	11.9
SPREAD	63.7	22.8	16.4	12	5.1
# LOSS YRS.	8	2	0	0	0

These criteria are intended for use with mutual fund investment systems with many Buy/Sell transactions per year. Most of the mutual fund investment systems discussed in this book employ such a market timing (mktime) model or system. These systems generate several Buy and Sell signals during each year. When a Buy signal is generated, assets are transferred from a money market fund to a growth fund. The reverse process occurs when a Sell signal is generated. A Buy/Sell transaction begins when a Buy signal is generated and is followed by a Sell signal. The transaction ends when the next Buy signal is generated. The mutual fund investment systems discussed had an average number of Buy/Sell transactions per year that ranged from zero (for Buy and Hold) to 17.

"Return" Performance Criteria

Table 15 lists the criteria for evaluating the past performance of mutual fund investment systems. Two criteria categories are shown: "return" criteria and "risk" criteria.

The "return" criteria indicate the average or mean performance during a period of ten or more years and includes:

- Mean Annualized Return (MAR) or compounded rate of return
- Average percentage of profitable Buy/Sell transactions
- Mean Buy/Sell Transaction Return

The most important criterion for selecting an investment system to achieve long-term growth is the mean annualized return (MAR). *Our primary goal as long-term investors is to select a system that has* ***significantly*** *outperformed the S&P 500 Index as measured by the MAR for the periods covering the latest five years and ten or more years.*

The other two criteria supplement the MAR in evaluating systems with more than two Buy/Sell transactions per year. All other criteria being equal, we look for systems with an average percentage of profitable transactions that is greater than 50%.

TABLE 15
PERFORMANCE CRITERIA FOR EVALUATING MUTUAL FUND INVESTMENT SYSTEM DURING A PERIOD OF TEN OR MORE YEARS

ITEM #	RETURN CRITERIA	RISK CRITERIA
1	MEAN ANNUALIZED RETURN (MAR)	MINIMUM ANNUAL RETURN OR MAXIMUM ANNUAL LOSS
2	AVERAGE PERCENTAGE PROFITABLE BUY/SELL TRANSACTIONS	MINIMUM PERCENTAGE PROFITABLE BUY/SELL TRANSACTIONS DURING THE LAST EIGHT TRANSACTIONS
3	MEAN BUY/SELL TRANSACTION RETURN	MINIMUM BUY/SELL TRANSACTION RETURN OR MAXIMUM TRANSACTION LOSS

"Risk" Criteria

Investment risk may be defined as the probability that the future return from an investment will differ from its expected value. In general, the greater the variation of past returns from the expected value, (i.e. the greater the volatility), the greater the risk.

Investment risk may be quantified by several different measures. Two of the most common measures of risk (that are used in the financial community) are beta and standard deviation.

Beta measures the volatility of a security or a mutual fund with respect to the volatility of the overall stock market; e.g., S&P 500 Index is set at 1.0. Securities that are more volatile than the index have betas greater than 1.0, if less volatile, betas are less than 1.0. If the index increases in value by 1.5%, a security with a beta of 1.2 will (on the average) increase in value by 1.8% (1.5 x 1.2).

Standard deviation measures the volatility of a security with respect to its expected value over a specified time period, namely its mean annualized return (MAR).. If a security has a 10-Year MAR of 15%, and a standard deviation of 3% over the same period, then 68% of the returns will lie in the range between 12% (15-3) and 18% (15+3) of its MAR. Moreover, 90% of the returns will lie in the range between 10.9% (15-4.1) and 19.1% (15+4.1). These statistics are based on the assumption that the returns vary according to a "normal" distribution.

Standard deviation and mean annualized return can be used to predict the worst case annual return of an investment vehicle based upon its past performance. In the past, we have used standard deviation as our measure of investment risk for two reasons: (1) it is readily calculated by individual investors and (2) it is useful in predicting the worst case return.

With the arrival of top-performing mktime models with high switching rates (i.e., more than two Buy/Sell transactions per year), we have been using "risk" criteria that an individual investor can use more effectively than beta or standard deviation. These criteria are based upon a statistical analysis of an investment system's performance during a period of ten or more years. These criteria are listed in Table 15 and are described below.

The "risk" criteria shown in Table 15 indicate worst case performance during a period of ten or more years and include:

- Minimum Annual Return or Maximum Annual Loss
- Minimum Percentage of Profitable Buy/Sell Transactions during the last eight transactions
- Maximum Buy/Sell Transaction Loss

These criteria may be used both for selecting an investment system as well as monitoring the selected system's performance subsequently. Given the choice of two systems with approximately the same 5-year and 10-year MAR values, the system with the best "risk" criteria values should be selected. The "risk" criteria may be used to monitor an investment system's performance as follows:

- *Maximum Transaction Loss.* If the loss during a Buy period (growth fund investment) exceeds this value, then switch *assets* to a money market fund before the generation of a Sell signal.
- *Minimum Percentage of Profitable Transactions.* If the percentage of profitable transactions during the last eight transactions drops below this value, then switch assets to a money market fund and remain there until the problem is diagnosed and corrected.
- *Maximum Annual Loss.* If the loss during a calendar year significantly exceeds this value, then switch assets to a money market fund and remain there until the problem is diagnosed and corrected.

Applying the "Return/Risk" Criteria

Chapter 6 describes the hypothetical past performance of the 1993 top-performing mutual fund investment systems using the "return" and "risk" described above.

Measuring Investment Growth

There are at least three methods for measuring investment growth: (1) mean annualized return (MAR); (2) total return during a specified time period; and (3) future value of a lump sum investment at the end of a specified time period.

Mean annualized return (MAR) is the same as the compounded rate of return. The compounded rate of return of a fixed-income investment measures how much a $1 lump sum investment grows during a specified time period. For example, the value of a fixed-income investment (yielding 7.5% per year) at the end of five years is equal to:

$1.075 x 1.075 x 1.075 x 1.075 x1.075 = $1.436

The annual returns of a growth mutual fund investment will vary. If a $1 lump sum investment in such a fund will grow at the end of N years to the same value as for a fixed-income investment, then the mutual fund has a MAR equal to the yield of the fixed-income investment. For example, the value of a growth fund investment (with the following annual returns) at the end of five years is equal to:

$1.10 x 1.05 x 1.12 x 1.02 x 1.088 = $1.436

Therefore, this growth fund investment has a mean annualized return of 7.5% since a $1 lump sum investment grew to $1.436; i.e., the same value as a fixed-income investment yielding 7.5% per year.

Total return is equal to the percentage increase in the value of a lump sum investment during a specified time period. The total return of the above described fixed-income and growth fund investments is equal to 43.6%.

The **future value** of a lump sum investment at the end of a specified period is equal to the initial lump sum investment augmented by the total return. In the above examples, the future value at the end of five years would be $1.436; at the end of ten years, the future value would be $2.061. To obtain a realistic future value, it is necessary to consider the impact of inflation. In other words, the value of future dollars in terms of purchasing power will be decreased as a result of inflation. Therefore, inflation-adjusted future value is computed as a realistic measure of investment growth. An inflation-adjusted future value will measure the growth of a tax-qualified investment, i.e., an investment wherein income taxes on earnings are deferred as in a pension plan or an IRA. If an investment is not covered by a tax-qualified plan, then the future value must be adjusted for both inflation and federal/state income taxes.

Total Return vs. Mean Annualized Return (MAR)

Tables 16 part A, and 16, part B indicate the variation of total investment return versus mean annualized return (for different holding periods) without and with adjustment for an inflation rate of 5%. Figure 4 illustrates the variation of ***inflation-adjusted*** total return for holding periods of 10,15 and 20 years. These tables and figure graphically show the power of what has been called the "eighth wonder of the world"; namely, compound interest. An individual starting an investment program at age 45 will have achieved an inflation-adjusted total return of **520%** when he/she retires at age 65 if the program provides a mean annualized return of 15%. This result is achieved if the federal/state income taxes were deferred. Figure 5 and Table 16, part C show the variation of total return, ***after adjustment for both inflation and taxes***, with mean annualized return. The above individual will achieve a total return of **180%** when he/she retires at age 65. Income tax deferral increases the total return by a factor of 2.9 from 180% to 520%.

Future Investment Value vs. Mean Annualized Return (MAR)

Tables 17A, and 17B show the future value of a lump sum investment adjustmented for an inflation rate of 5%. Figure 6 illustrates the variation of the inflation-adjusted future investment value for holding periods of 10,15 and 20 years. **These tables and figure indicate that the future *inflation-adjusted*** value for a holding period of 20 years is:

- $ 6,000 for MAR = 15%
- $14,000 for MAR = 20%
- $33,000 for MAR = 25%

Please note that the future inflation-adjusted value increases by a factor of approximately 2.3 as the MAR increases by 5% from 15% to 20% to 25%.

Figure 7 and Table 17C show the variation of future investment value (after adjustment for both inflation and income taxes) with mean annualized return. The figure and table indicate that the future investment value (***after adjustment for inflation and income taxes***) for a holding period of 20 years is:

- $2,800 for MAR = 15%
- $5,200 for MAR = 20%
- $9,500 for MAR = 25%

FIGURE 4

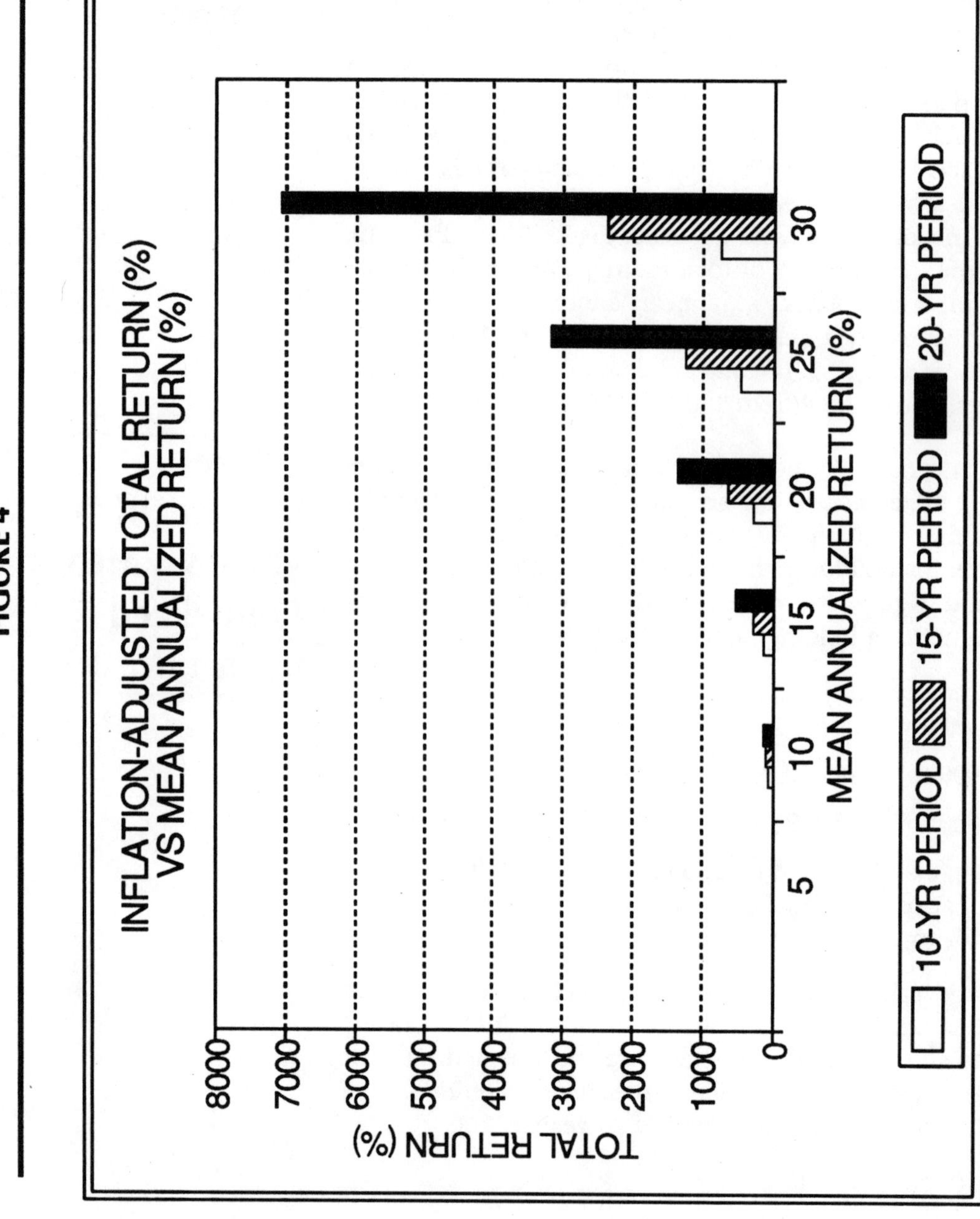
INFLATION-ADJUSTED TOTAL RETURN (%)
VS MEAN ANNUALIZED RETURN (%)
TOTAL RETURN (%)
8000
7000
6000
5000
4000
3000
2000
1000
0
5
10
15
20
25
30
MEAN ANNUALIZED RETURN (%)
10-YR PERIOD
15-YR PERIOD
20-YR PERIOD

TABLE 16
TOTAL INVESTMENT RETURN (%) VS HOLDING PERIOD (YRS) VS MEAN ANNUALIZED RETURN OR COMPOUNDED RATE OF RETURN

A. NO ADJUSTMENT FOR INFLATION AND/OR INCOME TAXES

HOLDING PERIOD [YRS]	MEAN ANNUALIZED RETURN OR COMPOUNDED RATE OF RETURN (%)						
	5	10	15	20	25	30	35
5	30	60	100	150	210	270	350
10	60	160	310	520	830	1300	1900
15	110	320	710	1400	2700	5000	8900
20	170	570	1500	3700	8600	19000	40000
25	240	980	3200	9400	26000	71000	181000
30	330	1700	6500	24000	81000	262000	813000
B. TOTAL RETURN ADJUSTED FOR 5% INFLATION							
5	0	30	60	100	140	190	250
10	0	60	150	280	470	750	1100
15	0	100	290	640	1300	2400	4200
20	0	150	520	1300	3200	7100	15000
25	0	220	870	2700	7700	21000	53000
30	0	300	1400	5400	19000	61000	188000

FIGURE 5

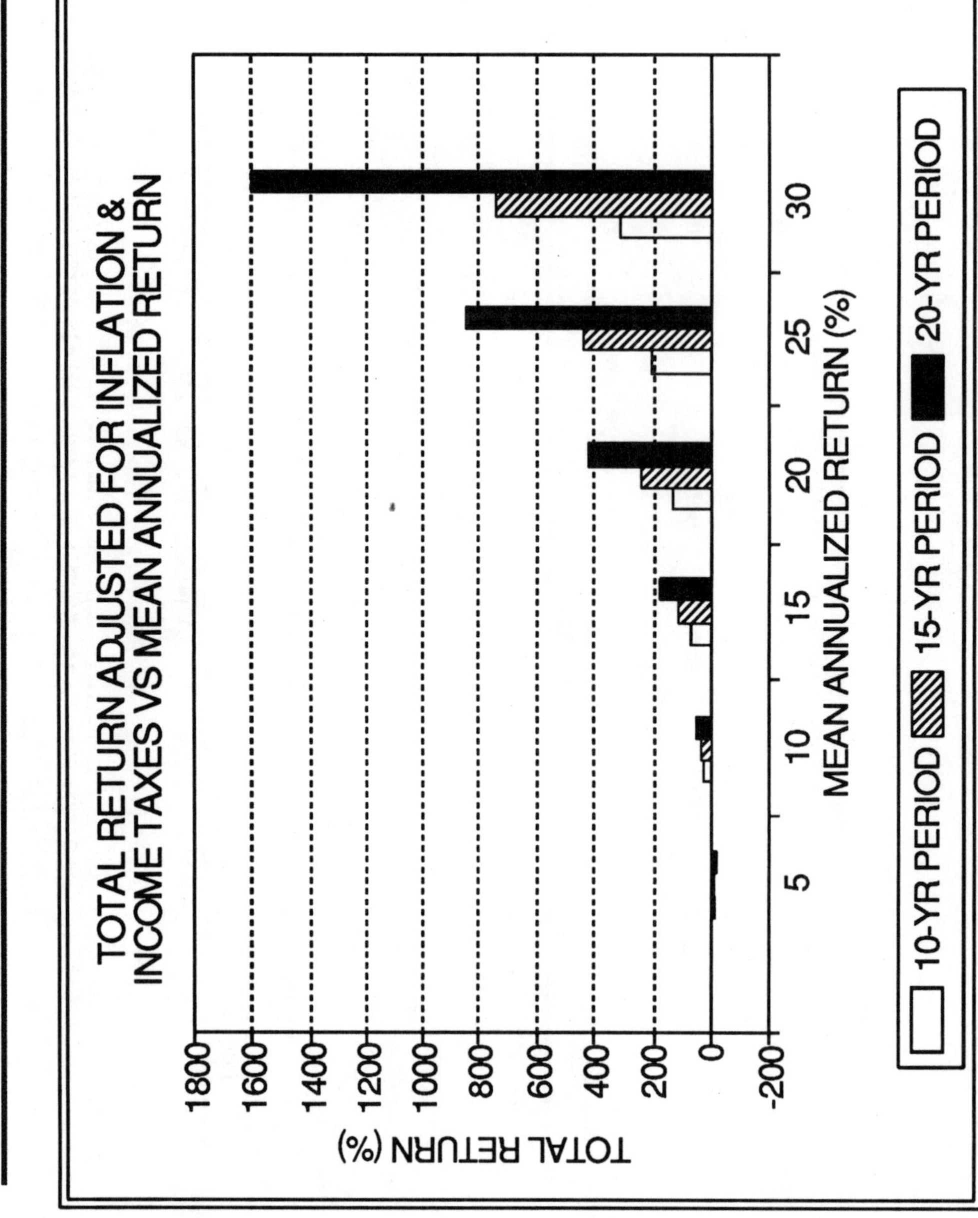
TOTAL RETURN ADJUSTED FOR INFLATION &
INCOME TAXES VS MEAN ANNUALIZED RETURN
TOTAL RETURN (%)
1800
1600
1400
1200
1000
800
600
400
200
0
-200
5
10
15
20
25
30
MEAN ANNUALIZED RETURN (%)
10-YR PERIOD
15-YR PERIOD
20-YR PERIOD

TABLE 16 (CONTINUED)
TOTAL INVESTMENT RETURN (%) VS HOLDING PERIOD (YRS) VS MEAN ANNUALIZED RETURN OR COMPOUNDED RATE OF RETURN

C. TOTAL RETURN ADJUSTED FOR INFLATION & INCOME TAXES HOLDING

HOLDING PERIOD [YRS]	MEAN ANNUALIZED RETURN OR COMPOUNDED RATE OF RETURN (%)						
	5	**10**	**15**	**20**	**25**	**30**	**35**
5	-7	10	30	50	75	100	130
10	-13	21	70	130	210	310	450
15	-19	33	115	240	440	740	1200
20	-25	46	180	420	850	1600	2900
25	-30	60	260	680	1600	3400	7000
30	-35	76	360	1100	2800	6900	16500

TABLE 17
FUTURE VALUE OF $1,000 LUMP SUM INVESTMENT ($000) VS MEAN ANNUALIZED RETURN OR COMPOUNDED RATE OF RETURN

HOLDING PERIOD [YRS]	MEAN ANNUALIZED RETURN OR COMPOUNDED RATE OF RETURN (%)						
	5	10	15	20	25	30	35
A. NO ADJUSTMENT FOR INFLATION AND/OR INCOME TAXES							
5	1.3	1.6	2.0	2.5	3.1	3.7	4.5
10	1.6	2.6	4.0	6.2	9.3	13.8	20.1
15	2.1	4.2	8.1	15.4	28.4	51.2	90.2
20	2.7	6.7	16.4	38.3	86.7	190	400
25	3.4	10.8	32.9	95.4	265	710	1800
30	4.3	17.4	66.2	240	810	2620	8100
B. FUTURE VALUE ADJUSTED FOR 5% INFLATION ($000)							
5	1.0	1.3	1.6	2.0	2.4	2.9	3.5
10	1.0	1.6	2.5	3.8	5.7	8.5	12.3
15	1.0	2.0	3.9	7.4	13.7	24.6	43.4
20	1.0	2.5	6.2	14.4	32.7	71.6	150
25	1.0	3.2	9.7	28.2	78.2	210	540
30	1.0	4.0	15.3	54.9	190	610	1880

FIGURE 6

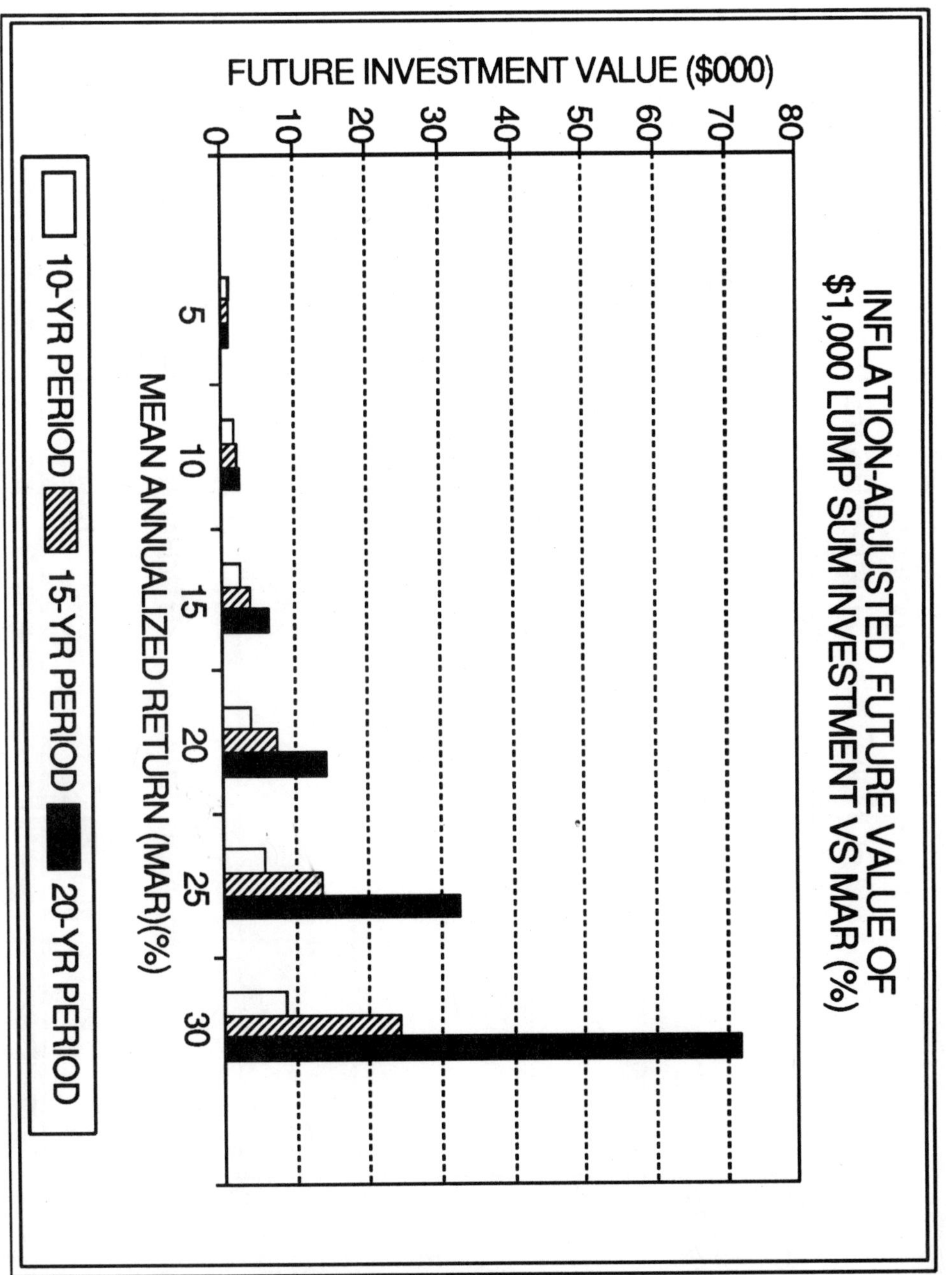
INFLATION-ADJUSTED FUTURE VALUE OF
$1,000 LUMP SUM INVESTMENT VS MAR (%)
FUTURE INVESTMENT VALUE ($000)
0
10
20
30
40
50
60
70
80
5
10
15
20
25
30
MEAN ANNUALIZED RETURN (MAR)(%)
10-YR PERIOD
15-YR PERIOD
20-YR PERIOD

FIGURE 7

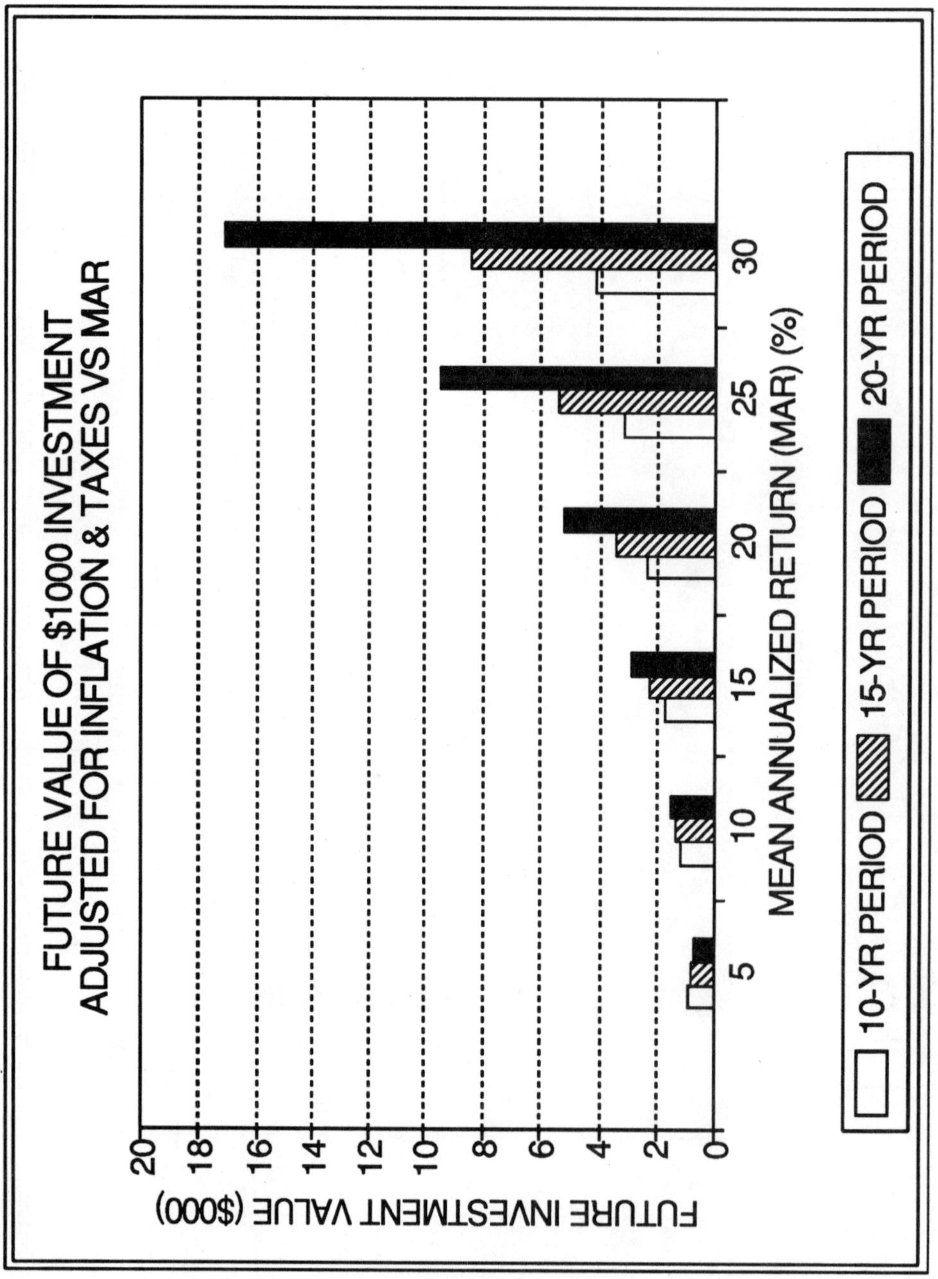

FUTURE VALUE OF $1000 INVESTMENT
ADJUSTED FOR INFLATION & TAXES VS MAR
FUTURE INVESTMENT VALUE ($000)
0
2
4
6
8
10
12
14
16
18
20
5
10
15
20
25
30
MEAN ANNUALIZED RETURN (MAR) (%)
10-YR PERIOD
15-YR PERIOD
20-YR PERIOD

TABLE 17 (CONTINUED)
FUTURE VALUE OF $1,000 LUMP SUM INVESTMENT VS MEAN ANNUALIZED RETURN OR COMPOUNDED RATE OF RETURN

C. FUTURE VALUE ADJUSTED FOR INFLATION & INCOME TAXES ($000)*

HOLDING PERIOD [YRS]	MEAN ANNUALIZED RETURN OR COMPOUNDED RATE OF RETURN (%)						
	5	**10**	**15**	**20**	**25**	**30**	**35**
5	0.9	1.1	1.3	1.5	1.8	2.0	2.3
10	0.9	1.2	1.7	2.3	3.1	4.1	5.5
15	0.8	1.3	2.2	3.4	5.4	8.4	12.9
20	0.7	1.5	2.8	5.2	9.5	17.1	30.2
25	0.7	1.6	3.6	7.8	16.6	34.7	70.7
30	0.6	1.8	4.6	11.8	29.2	70.5	170

* Assuming a total federal/state income tax rate of 30% on investment returns.

3: OVERALL APPROACH

Investment Objective

Our objective in selecting and in investing in the top-performing, mutual fund investment systems is to achieve substantial, long-term growth with a minimum of risk. By substantial growth, we mean a compounded rate of return, i.e., mean annualized return (MAR), that is significantly greater than the MAR achieved by the S&P 500 Index during the same time period. By long term, we mean a period of ten or more years.

During the 11-year period from 1982 through 1992, the S&P 500 Index achieved a MAR of 16.7%. The inflation-adjusted total return during the 11-year period was 220% after adjustment for a 5% inflation rate. A lump sum investment of $1,000 in the index on December 31, 1981, would have grown to $3,200 on December 31, 1992, after adjustment for a 5% inflation rate. As indicated above, our objective is to select investment systems that achieve performance results significantly greater than these S&P 500 Index performance results.

Risk can be defined in many different ways. In Chapter 2, we described three "risk" criteria for use in evaluating the past performance of mutual fund investment systems. The most basic criterion is the minimum annual return over a period of ten or more years. The minimum annual return of the S&P 500 Index (with dividends reinvested) during the 11-year period from 1982 through 1992 was -3.1%.

Basic Premises

The overall investment approach described in this report rests upon two basic premises:

(1) the investment system uses precisely defined rules and

(2) past performance during a period of five or more years is a guide but *not a guarantee* of future performance.

Each of the mutual fund investment systems (which are candidates for selection as top performers) uses precisely defined rules for (1) generating Buy/Sell signals by using a mktime model, and (2) selecting the best growth fund when a Buy signal is generated. The past performance of these systems can therefore be determined by computer back-testing using these precisely defined rules. The performance data presented in this report is obtained by computer back-testing (rather than actual investment) and is therefore considered as hypothetical data.

Evolution of the Investment Strategy

The approach that we describe below (for selecting top-performing mutual fund investment systems) was developed by the Association of Mutual Fund Investors (AMFI) during the past seven years (1986 through 1992). AMFI is an independent, non-profit corporation that conducts program of investment research, education and information dissemination. During the 7-year period from 1986 to 1992, AMFI operated as the AAII Philadelphia Mutual Funds Special Interest Group (MFG).

Our investment approach has evolved during the past seven years through three phases as described below and in Table 18A. We anticipate that our continuing mutual fund investment research will provide investment systems with improved returns and/or lower risks.

Investment Strategy

Phase I

In Phase I, an individual investor buys and holds an S&P 500 Index fund such as the Vanguard Index 500 fund. During the 11-year period from 1982 through 1992, the S&P 500 Index achieved a MAR of 16.7%. As indicated before, and in Figure 1, an average of 59% of U.S. professional money managers ***under-performed*** the index during the 10-year period from 1982 through 1991. In other words, the performance of the index represents a high standard of investment performance. The worst-case annual return of the index during the 11-year period was -3.1%.

Phase II

In Phase II, the individual investor employs an S&P 500 Index fund that can be switched to a money market fund and vice versa at least 12 times a year. Such switching may be made directly through the fund or indirectly through a mutual fund trading broker. The fund is used in conjunction with a top-performing market timing (mktime) model. The model employs precisely defined rules to generate Buy or Sell signals. A Buy signal indicates that assets should be transferred from a money market fund into the index fund. A Sell signal indicates that a reverse transfer should occur; i.e., assets should be transferred from the index fund to a money market fund.

During the 11-year period from 1982 through 1992, the S&P 500 Index fund when timed by the top-performing mktime model (See Chapter 4) would have achieved a **MAR of 23.2%** in Phase II. The financial significance of increasing the 11-year MAR from 16.7% to 23.2% is shown in Figures 8A and 8B and and below:

- The *inflation-adjusted* total return (during the 11-year period) increased by 2.2 times from 220% to 480%.
- The *inflation-adjusted* future value of a $1000 lump sum investment made on 12/31/81 increased by 1.8 times from $3,200 to $5,800.
- The investment risk would have decreased since the worst-case annual return increased from -3.1% to 1.9%.

Phase III

In Phase III, the individual investor has become more experienced and, as a result, more confident in his/her investment strategy. Instead of employing an index fund, he/she uses a growth fund selection system (Chapter 5) in conjunction with a top-performing mktime model (Chapter 4). When a Buy signal is generated, the growth fund selection system (GFSS) determines the best growth fund for investment during the forthcoming Buy cycle.

During the 11-year period from 1982 through 1992, the hypothetical MAR achieved by the top-performing GFSS-selected growth fund (when timed by the top-performing mktime model) was **38.3%**. The financial significance of increasing the 11-year MAR from 16.7% in Phase I to 38.3% in Phase III is shown in Figures 8A and 8B and Table 18B and below:

- The **Inflation-adjusted** total return increased by 8.9 times from 220% to 1,970%.

TABLE 18A
EVOLUTION OF AMFI MUTUAL FUND INVESTMENT STRATEGY

PHASE	INVESTMENT SYSTEM: GROWTH FUND OR GFSS (NOTE 1)	INVESTMENT SYSTEM: MKTIME MODEL	MAR (%) (82-92)	ANNUALIZED RETURNS (%) [1982-1992]: MAXIMUM	ANNUALIZED RETURNS (%) [1982-1992]: MINIMUM
I	S&P 500 INDEX FUND	BUY & HOLD	16.7	31.8	-3.1
II	S&P 500 INDEX FUND	TOP-PERFORMING MKTIME MODEL (NOTE 2)	23.2	37.4	1.9
III	TOP-PERFORMING GROWTH FUND SELECTION SYSTEM (NOTE 1)	TOP-PERFORMING MKTIME MODEL (NOTE 2)	38.3	72.0	13.0

NOTES:
1. GFSS = GROWTH FUND SELECTION SYSTEM. GFSS2 IS THE TOP-PERFORMING GROWTH FUND SELECTION SYSTEM. SEE CHAPTER 5.
2. MTM6 WAS THE TOP-PERFORMING MKTIME MODEL. SEE CHAPTER 4.

FIGURE 8A

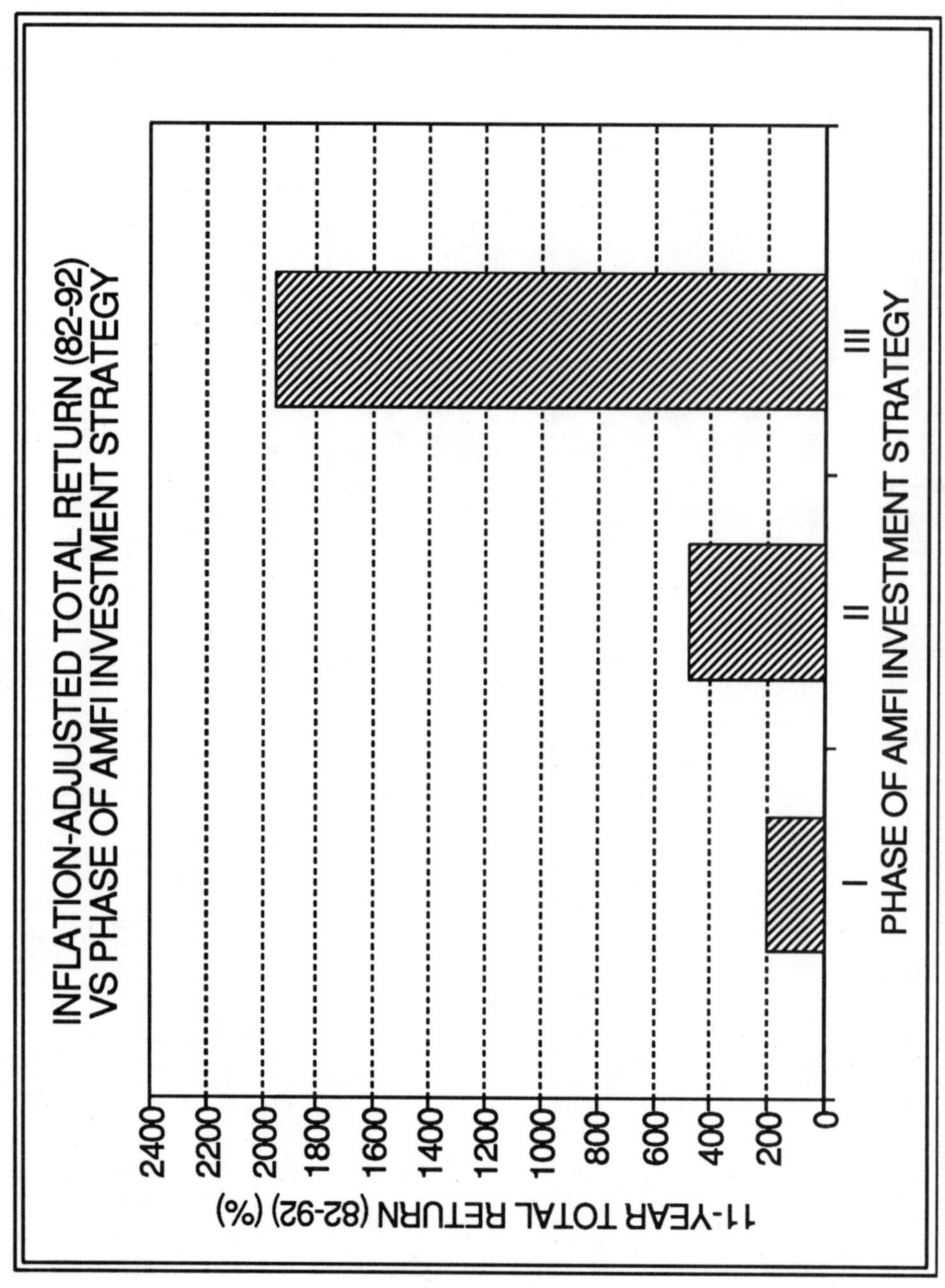
INFLATION-ADJUSTED TOTAL RETURN (82-92)
VS PHASE OF AMFI INVESTMENT STRATEGY
11-YEAR TOTAL RETURN (82-92) (%)
2400
2200
2000
1800
1600
1400
1200
1000
800
600
400
200
0
I
II
III
PHASE OF AMFI INVESTMENT STRATEGY

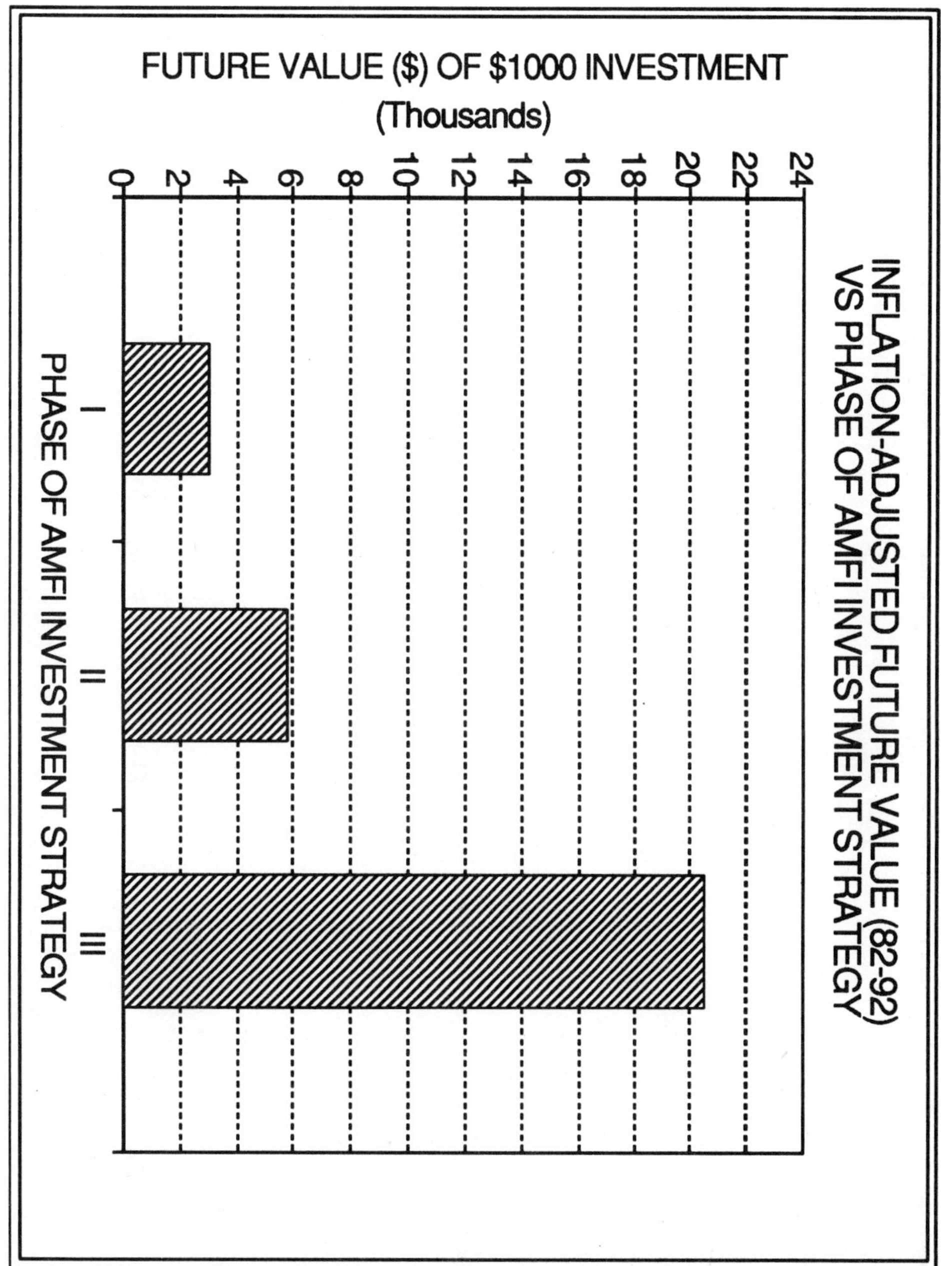
INFLATION-ADJUSTED FUTURE VALUE (82-92)
VS PHASE OF AMFI INVESTMENT STRATEGY
FUTURE VALUE ($) OF $1000 INVESTMENT
(Thousands)
0
2
4
6
8
10
12
14
16
18
20
22
24
I
II
III
PHASE OF AMFI INVESTMENT STRATEGY

FIGURE 8B

TABLE 18B
HYPOTHETICAL INVESTMENT PERFORMANCE OF THE THREE PHASES OF AMFI INVESTMENT STRATEGY DURING THE 11-YEAR PERIOD FROM 1982 TO 1992

PHASE	INFLATION-ADJUSTED @ 5%/YR		
	MEAN ANNUALIZED RETURN (%)	TOTAL 11-YR RETURN (%)	FUTURE VALUE ($) (NOTE 1)
I	16.7	220	3,200
II	23.2	480	5,800
III	38.2	1,970	20,700

NOTES: 1. FUTURE VALUE ON 12/31/92 IS BASED UPON A LUMP SUM INVESTMENT OF $1,000 ON 12/31/81.

- The **Inflation-adjusted** future value of a $1,000 lump sum investment (made on 12/31/81) increased by 6.4 times from $3,200 to $20,700.
- The investment risk would have decreased since the worst-case annual return increased from -3.1% to 13%.

Continuous Investment Research

In order to develop and/or evaluate better top-performing investment systems, AMFI performs mutual fund investment research on a continuous basis. In 1992, we developed an improved growth fund selection system for use with several of the top-performing mktime models. In 1993, we expect to develop and/or evaluate one or more improved mktime models.

To educate its members, AMFI publishes a bimonthly newsletter that describes the results of its investment research. This newsletter is distributed to AMFI members one week before the AMFI bimonthly meetings. At these meetings, the tables and charts in the newsletter are presented to explain the investment research described and to stimulate discussion and interaction.

Investment System Selection Process

Table 19 summarizes the four step process that we use to determine the top-performing mutual fund investment systems for use during 1993.

In Step 1, we select the five top-performing models (during the previous 5-year period from 1988 through 1992) from 45 candidate mktime models as described in Section 4. These candidate models include mktime newsletters, audited money managers using market timing and AMFI-generated models. The candidate models are ranked by the 5-year performance of the S&P 500 Index when timed by each model.

In Step 2, we select (during the 11-year period from 1982 through 1992) the best growth fund for use with each mktime model when the model generated a Buy signal. We use a growth fund selection system (as described in Chapter 5) to select the best growth fund for use with three of the five top-performing mktime models. The S&P 500 Index is used with the other two top-performing models.

In Step 3, we compute the 11-year returns for the S&P 500 Index and the five top-performing investment systems during the 11-

TABLE 19
THE FOUR-STEP PROCESS TO DETERMINE THE 1993 TOP-PERFORMING MUTUAL FUND INVESTMENT SYSTEMS AND THE 1993 SYSTEM MOST SUITABLE FOR YOU AND YOUR INVESTMENTS

STEP 1: **MKTIME MODEL SELECTION (SECTION 4)**

DETERMINE THE FIVE (5) TOP-PERFORMING MKTIME MODELS DURING THE PREVIOUS FIVE YEARS (1988-1992).

STEP 2: **GROWTH FUND SELECTION (SECTION 5)**

WHEN A SELECTED MKTIME MODEL GENERATES A BUY SIGNAL DURING THE 11-YEAR PERIOD FROM 1982 THROUGH 1992, USE THE ASSOCIATED GROWTH FUND SELECTION SYSTEM TO SELECT THE BEST GROWTH FUND FOR SUCH MKTIME MODEL.

STEP 3: **SYSTEM PERFORMANCE COMPUTATION & EVALUATION (SECTION 6).**

- COMPUTE THE 11-YEAR RETURNS FOR THE S&P 500 INDEX AND THE FIVE INVESTMENT SYSTEMS THAT CONSIST OF A SELECTED MKTIME MODEL AND ASSOCIATED GROWTH FUND SELECTION SYSTEM.

- COMPUTE THE SYSTEM PERFORMANCE FIGURES-OF MERIT USING THE EVALUATION CRITERIA (DESCRIBED IN SECTION 2.5) FOR THE S&P 500 INDEX AND THE FIVE TOP-PERFORMING INVESTMENT SYSTEMS DURING THE 11-YEAR PERIOD.

STEP 4: **INVESTMENT SYSTEM RANKING AND SELECTION (SECTION 7).**

- RANK THE S&P 500 INDEX AND THE FIVE TOP-PERFORMING INVESTMENT SYSTEMS BY THEIR PERFORMANCE FIGURES-OF-MERIT.

- SELECT THE INVESTMENT SYSTEM MOST SUITABLE FOR YOU AND YOUR INVESTMENTS.

year period from 1982 through 1992. These systems consist of a top-performing mktime model and an associated growth fund selection system. The results of these computations are presented in Chapter 6 and are used to determine the performance figures-of-merit for each system. Performance criteria are described in Chapter 2.

In Step 4, we rank the S&P 500 Index and the five top-performing investment systems by their performance figures-of-merit; e.g., mean annualized return; minimum annual return or maximum annual loss; maximum Buy/Sell transaction loss, etc. On the basis of this ranking, we describe how an individual investor can select the investment system most suitable for his/her investments.

Implementing the Selected Investment System

Now that an individual investor has selected a top-performing mutual fund investment system, how does he/she make investments according to the system's Buy/Sell signals and growth fund selections? Table 20 outlines the alternate methods for implementing your selected, top-performing mutual fund investment system. Chapter 8 discusses these methods in greater detail.

TABLE 20
ALTERNATE METHODS OF
IMPLEMENTING YOUR SELECTED MUTUAL FUND INVESTMENT SYSTEM

1. **DO-IT-YOURSELF BY:**
   - BECOMING AN AMFI MEMBER
   - INSTALLING THE REQUIRED SOFTWARE ON YOUR PC
   - ENTERING SOFTWARE INPUT DATA DAILY OR WEEKLY SO AS TO GENERATE BUY/SELL SIGNALS & SELECT THE BEST GROWTH FUND(S)

2. **SUBSCRIBE TO A NON-AMFI NEWSLETTER AND ASSOCIATED HOTLINE THAT PROVIDES:**
   - DAILY BUY/SELL SIGNALS
   - GROWTH FUND SELECTION WHEN A BUY SIGNAL IS GENERATED

3. **BECOME A CLIENT OF A REGISTERED INVESTMENT ADVISER WHO:**
   - MANAGES CLIENT'S INVESTMENT ACCOUNTS
   - USES THE AMFI TOP-PERFORMING SYSTEMS

4. **FORM AN INVESTMENT CLUB THAT USES METHODS 1,2 OR 3**

4: SELECTING THE TOP-PERFORMING MKTIME MODELS

Overview

The first of the four steps in the investment systems selection process is the annual selection of the five top-performing mktime models. These mktime models are selected from mktime model candidates that outperformed the S&P 500 Index (when bought and held) when timing the index during the preceding five years. The mktime model candidates are obtained from three sources that objectively evaluate the past performance of various categories of mktime models. These sources are listed in Table 21.

Hulbert Financial Digest is a newsletter that evaluates the past performance of stock and mutual fund newsletters. The performance of newsletters that provide market timing advice is evaluated by the results obtained when timing the Wilshire 5000 Index.

The MoniResearch Newsletter evaluates the past performance of professional money managers that employ market timing. The past performance is based upon the results obtained when timing the S&P 500 Index.

Performance Evaluation Criteria

The mktime models are evaluated on the basis of the long-term performance rating (LPR) of the S&P 500 Index when timed by the mktime models as compared with the LPR of the index when bought and held. LPR is defined as the mean (or geometric average) of the 5-year and 2-year mean annualized returns (MAR). As previously indicated, MAR is the same as the compounded annual rate of return.

The MAR and LPR values are computed using the net annual returns of the index when timed. The net annual return is equal to the gross annual return less the annual mutual fund trading fees or commissions where applicable. These fees are applicable when a mutual fund trading broker is employed. Such a broker is needed to switch rapidly assets:

(1) from one mutual fund to another in the same family of funds more than four times per year and/or,

TABLE 21
MKTIME MODEL CANDIDATES FOR SELECTION AS THE FIVE TOP-PERFORMING MKTIME MODELS

	MKTIME MIODEL CATEGORY		
#	INFORMATION SOURCE	APPROX. QUANTITY OF MODELS	DATA AVAILABILITY [1]
1	ASSOCIATION OF MUTUAL FUND INVESTORS (AMFI)	5	EARLY JANUARY
2	HULBERT FINANCIAL DIGEST	20	MARCH
3	MONIRESEARCH NEWSLETTER	20	APRIL

NOTES:
1. DATE SHOWN INDICATES WHEN THE PERFORMANCE DATA FOR THE FIVE PREVIOUS YEARS IS AVAILABLE. THIS DATA IS USED TO SELECT THE TOP-PERFORMING MKTIME MODEL(S) IN THE CATEGORY.

(2) from one mutual fund family to another.

Mutual fund trading brokers include Charles Schwab, Waterhouse Securities and Jack White & Company. As far as we know, the lowest trading fees are available at this time from Jack White & Company (800-233-3411) and its subsidiary, Shareholder Services Corporation. Jack White & Company handles individual investor accounts while Shareholder Services Corporation handles institutional accounts. Their trading fees are described in Appendix G. In the performance data presented in this report, we have assumed a trading fee of 0.17% for a single, one-way transfer from a growth fund to a money market fund or vice versa.

Availability of Mktime Model Performance Data

Table 21 indicates that the AMFI data is available in early January whereas the other data is not available until March and April. Since this book was prepared in January 1993, only the AMFI mktime model data was available for selection of the **1993** top-performing mktime models and is described below. However, to illustrate the complete process of mktime model selection, we will also describe the selection of the **1992** top-performing mktime models.

The AMFI Mktime Models

Table 22 lists the five AMFI mktime models (designated as MTM2 through MTM6) that have been developed and/or evaluated during the 7-year period of AMFI's operations from 1986 to 1992. Buy/Hold (i.e. no market timing) is designated as MTM1. Table 22 briefly describes each mktime model and refers to Appendices B through F for additional information.

1992 Mktime Model Selection

Table 23A indicates the hypothetical performance results for the S&P 500 Index (when timed by the five AMFI mktime models and when bought and held) during the 5-year period from 1987 through 1991. Therefore, this data would be used for selecting the 1992 top-performing mktime models.

Table 23A also shows the net annual returns during each of the five years. From these annual returns, we compute (as discussed below) the 2-year and 5-year mean annualized returns. From these annualized returns, we compute the 5-year long-

TABLE 22
THE FIVE 1992 & 1993 AMFI MKTIME MODELS COMPARATIVE CHARACTERISTICS

MKTIME MODEL ID	MKTIME MODEL DESCRIPTION	DATA INPUT FREQUENCY	AVG # SWITCHES PER YEAR	S&P 500 LPR DURING 5-YR PERIOD ENDING ON 12/31/	
				1991	1992
MTM1	BUY & HOLD TOP-PERFORMING GROWTH FUNDS	WEEKLY	0	13.9	17.2
MTM2	S&P 500 DIVIDEND YIELD IS EMPLOYED AS THE SOLE MKTIME INDICATOR (SEE APPENDIX B).	WEEKLY	0.4	16.9	15.8
MTM3	FOUR MKTIME INDICATORS ARE EMPLOYED TO GENERATE BUY OR SELL SIGNALS. THE INDICATORS INCLUDE THE S&P 500 DIVIDEND YIELD AND TWO 39-WEEK MOVING AVERAGES (SEE APPENDIX C).	WEEKLY	1.7	17.1	15.4
MTM4	TWO SEASONALITY INDICATORS (END-OF-MONTH AND HOLIDAY) ARE EMPLOYED TO GENERATE BUY/SELL SIGNALS. (SEE APPENDIX D).	NA	33	14.9	5.5
MTM5	AIQ MARKET EXPERT SOFTWARE SYSTEM, VERSION 3.5.1. THIS SYSTEM EMPLOYS ABOUT 25 MKTIME INDICATORS WHICH ARE WEIGHTED TO GENERATE BUY OR SELL SIGNALS. THIS SYSTEM IS AVAILABLE FROM AIQ SYSTEMS, INC. (800-332-2999) AND IS EXECUTED ON A PC (APPENDIX E).	DAILY	11	21.1	16.4
MTM6	THIS MODEL COMBINES MODIFIED VERSIONS OF THE MTM4 AND MTM5 MKTIME MODELS. THE MODIFICATIONS ARE DETERMINED BY COMPUTER BACK-TESTING OVER PERIODS FROM 5 TO 12 YEARS. (SEE APPENDIX F).	DAILY	13	24.6	18.2

TABLE 23A
PERFORMANCE RESULTS FOR S&P 500 INDEX WHEN TIMED BY THE FIVE AMFI MKTIME MODELS DURING 5-YEAR PERIOD FROM 1987 TO 1991

		NET ANNUAL RETURNS [%]							
LPR RANK	MARKET TIMING MODEL (NOTE 1)	1991	1990	1989	1988	1987	5-YR MAR [2]	2-YR MAR [2]	LPR [3]
1	MTM6 (MTM5 + MTM4)*	33.5	11.7	32.6	22.0	37.6	27.1	22.1	24.6
2	MTM5 (AIQ SOFTWARE)*	30.7	11.2	27.4	13.8	26.5	21.7	20.6	21.1
3	MTM3 (MVG AVERAGES PLUS)	28.9	-0.4	30.6	16.4	33.1	21.0	13.3	17.1
4	MTM2 (S&P 500 DVD YLD)	30.5	-3.1	31.7	16.6	36.0	21.4	12.5	16.9
5	MTM4 (SEASONALITY)*	7.4	16.6	19.3	24.7	22.3	17.9	11.9	14.9
	MTM1 (BUY/HOLD)	30.5	-3.1	31.7	16.6	5.2	15.4	12.5	13.9

NOTES:

1. SEE TABLE 22 FOR DESCRIPTION OF MKTIME MODELS.
2. MAR = MEAN ANNUALIZED RETURN OR COMPOUNDED RATE OF RETURN.
3. LPR = LONG-TERM PERFORMANCE RATING = MEAN (OR GEOMETRIC AVERAGE) OF 5-YR MAR AND 2-YR MAR.
4. * INDICATES THAT THE ANNUAL RETURNS HAVE BEEN ADJUSTED FOR MUTUAL FUND TRADING FEES.

TABLE 23B
PERFORMANCE RESULTS FOR S&P 500 INDEX WHEN TIMED BY THE FIVE AMFI MKTIME MODELS DURING 5-YEAR PERIOD FROM 1988 TO 1992

LPR RANK	MARKET TIMING MODEL (NOTE 1)	NET ANNUAL RETURNS (%) 1992	1991	1990	1989	1988	5-YR MAR (2)	2-YR MAR (2)	LPR (3)
1	MTM6 (MTM5 + MTM4)*	1.9	33.5	11.7	32.6	22.0	19.7	16.6	18.2
2	MTM5 (AIQ SOFTWARE)*	3.1	30.7	11.2	27.4	13.8	16.8	16.1	16.4
3	MTM3 (MVG AVERAGES PLUS)	4.0	30.5	-3.1	31.7	16.6	15.1	16.5	15.8
4	MTM2 (S&P 500 DVD YLD)	3.8	28.9	-0.4	30.6	16.4	15.2	15.7	15.4
5	MTM4 (SEASONALITY)*	-7.2	7.4	16.6	19.3	24.7	11.6	-0.2	5.5
	MTM1 (BUY/HOLD)	7.7	30.5	-3.1	31.7	16.6	15.9	18.6	17.2

NOTES:

1. SEE TABLE 22 FOR DESCRIPTION OF MKTIME MODELS.
2. MAR = MEAN ANNUALIZED RETURN OR COMPOUNDED RATE OF RETURN.
3. LPR = LONG-TERM PERFORMANCE RATING = MEAN (OR GEOMETRIC AVERAGE) OF 5-YR MAR AND 2-YR MAR.
4. * INDICATES THAT THE ANNUAL RETURNS HAVE BEEN ADJUSTED FOR MUTUAL FUND TRADING FEES.

term performance rating (LPR). The mktime model performance is evaluated on the basis of their LPR values.

The 2-year MAR (mean annualized return) is the mean (or geometric average) of the annual returns during the previous two years; i.e., 1991 and 1990. For example, the 2-year MAR of the MTM6-timed index is equal to the *square root* of the product of the 1991 and 1992 annual returns, as shown:

$$2MAR = \sqrt{1.335 \cdot 1.117} = 1.221$$

Note that the annual returns are expressed as the ratio of the asset market value at the end of the year to the market value at the beginning of the year. For example, if a $1,000 investment at the beginning of a year yields $1,180 at the end of the year, then the return (expressed as a ratio) is 1.18. The percentage return is 18%.

The 5-year MAR is the mean of the annual returns during the 5-year period. For example, the 5-year MAR of the MTM6-timed index is equal to the *5th root* of the 5 annual returns:

$$5MAR = \sqrt[5]{1.335 \cdot 1.117 \cdot 1.326 \cdot 1.22 \cdot 1.376} = 1.271$$

The LPR is the mean of the 2-year MAR and the 5-year MAR. For example, the 5-year LPR of the MTM6-timed index is equal to the *square root* of 2MAR and 5 MAR:

$$LPR = \sqrt{1.271 \cdot 1.221} = 1.246$$

Table 23A indicates that:

- All five AMFI mktime models yielded LPR values greater than the Buy/Hold LPR by margins from 1% to 11%.
- The MTM6 mktime model generated the highest LPR value (24.6%) or 10.7% greater than Buy/Hold (at 13.9%) during the 5-year period from 1987 through 1991.

We selected all five AMFI mktime models as candidates for subsequent consideration as the five top-performing 1992 mktime models because:

- Each model outperformed Buy/Hold.
- 11-year performance data is readily available.

1993 Mktime Model Selection

Table 23B provides the same hypothetical performance results as Table 23A except that the 5-year period is from 1988 through 1992. Therefore, this data would be used for selecting the preliminary 1993 top-performing mktime models.

Table 23B indicates that:

- Only one mktime model (MTM6) outperformed Buy/Hold on the basis of LPR values.
- Two mktime models (MTM6 and MTM5) outperformed Buy/Hold on the basis of 5-year MAR values.
- However, as indicated in Table 53, three mktime models (MTM6, MTM5 and MTM4) significantly outperformed the S&P 500 Index when these models are used with the GFSS2 growth fund selection system during the same 5-year period.

Mktime Newsletters

The *Hulbert Financial Digest* tracks the performance of over 150 investment newsletters. The January 1992 issue of the *Digest* listed 106 newsletters that provided market timing advice. However, annual returns for the 5-year period from 1987 through 1991 were available for only 19 of those newsletters that switched to cash equivalents (such as money market funds) when a Sell signal was generated. Table 24A lists these 19 newsletters with performance data for the Wilshire 5000 Index when timed by these 19 newsletters during the 5-year period from 1987 through 1991. Table 24A shows performance results that have **not** been adjusted for mutual fund trading fees. In the table, the newsletters are ranked by their LPR values.

Table 24B shows performance results for three of the four mktime newsletters that outperformed the Wilshire 5000 Index when bought and held. These performance results have been adjusted for mutual fund trading fees.

To select the 1992 top-performing mktime models, we need LPR data for each candidate when timing the S&P 500 Index rather than the Wilshire 5000 Index. We obtained (from the *Hulbert Financial Digest*) the Buy/Sell signals for the *Systems &*

TABLE 24A
PERFORMANCE RESULTS WITHOUT ADJUSTMENT FOR MUTUAL FUND TRADING FEES(1)
WILSHIRE 5000 VALUE-WEIGHTED INDEX WHEN TIMED BY MUTUAL FUND/STOCK NEWSLETTERS DURING 5-YEAR PERIOD FROM 1987 TO 1991

LPR		ANNUAL RETURNS (%)					MAR (%)		
RANK	NEWSLETTER-TIMING SYSTEM	1991	1990	1989	1988	1987	2-YR MAR	5-YR MAR	LPR (%)
1	SYSTEMS/FORECASTS-TIME TRND	31.3	4.3	28.8	25.5	13.9	17.0	20.3	18.7
2	INVESTORS INTELLIGENCE-SW FD	28.0	8.1	15.9	10.1	32.7	17.6	18.6	18.1
3	GRANVILLE MARKET LETTER	33.1	8.0	30.3	17.1	-17.1	19.9	12.7	16.2
4	INVESTECH MUTUAL FD ADVISOR	24.2	7.7	8.2	8.6	12.2	15.7	12.0	13.8
	BUY/HOLD WILSHIRE INDEX	34.2	-6.2	29.2	17.9	2.3	12.2	14.4	13.3
5	TELEPHONE SWITCH NEWSLETTER	35.3	-7.9	29.2	2.8	19.6	11.6	14.6	13.1
6	MARKET LOGIC	30.6	-6.2	29.2	17.9	7.4	10.7	14.9	12.8
7	MUTUAL FUND FORECASTER	30.4	-6.2	29.2	17.9	2.3	10.6	13.8	12.2
8	VALUE LINE INVESTMENT SURVEY	27.5	-2.7	23.3	17.3	2.3	11.4	12.9	12.1
9	DOW THEORY LETTERS	12.8	7.6	5.8	6.8	35.4	10.2	13.2	11.7
10	ZWEIG FORECAST-NO SHORTING	15.6	4.0	14.5	7.1	24.2	9.6	12.9	11.2
11	FUND EXCHANGE-FD TIMG MODEL	18.9	2.3	13.0	4.8	20.3	10.3	11.6	11.0
12	STOCKMKT CYCLES-MF SW ADVCE	12.5	5.0	13.1	6.2	27.6	8.7	12.6	10.6
13	MUTUAL FUND STRATEGIST	12.8	2.0	22.4	2.4	30.3	7.3	13.4	10.3
14	PROF. TAPE READER-MF TIMING	12.4	7.8	8.2	3.8	17.9	10.1	9.9	10.0
15	WEBER'S FUND ADVISOR	14.1	-1.5	28.0	17.5	2.3	7.6	12.2	9.9
16	GARSIDE FORECAST-BELL RINGR	16.3	-1.2	7.5	15.5	12.5	7.2	9.9	8.6
17	ELLIOT WAVE THEORIST-INVSTR	5.5	2.7	8.2	6.8	33.9	4.1	10.9	7.4
18	DINES LETTER	13.1	-6.5	21.4	10.2	15.2	2.8	10.3	6.5
19	BOB NUROCK'S ADVISORY	5.5	3.5	13.4	17.9	2.3	4.5	8.4	6.4

1. PERFORMANCE RESULTS ARE BASED ON THE ANNUAL RETURNS IN THE 1/92 HULBERT FINANCIAL DIGEST.

TABLE 24 (CONTINUED)
PERFORMANCE RESULTS ADJUSTED FOR MUTUAL FUND TRADING FEES DURING 5-YEAR PERIOD FROM 1987 TO 1991

B. WILSHIRE 5000 VALUE-WEIGHTED INDEX WHEN TIMED BY TOP THREE MKTIME NEWSLETTERS									
		ANNUAL RETURNS [%]					MEAN ANNUALIZED RETURN [MAR] [%]		
LPR RANK	NEWSLETTER-TIMING SYSTEM	1991	1990	1989	1988	1987	2-YR MAR	5-YR MAR	LPR (%) (2)
1	INVESTORS INTELLIGENCE SW FD	27.4	7.5	15.7	9.5	32.1	17.0	18.0	17.5
2	GRANVILLE MARKET LETTER	33.0	7.8	30.1	17.0	-17.8	19.7	12.4	16.0
3	SYSTEMS/FORECASTS-TIME TREND	29.9	0.6	26.1	21.4	12.4	14.3	17.6	15.9
C. S&P 500 INDEX WHEN TIMED BY THE TOP-PERFORMING MKTIME NEWSLETTER (NOTE 3)									
INVESTORS INTELLIGENCE		23.8	8.6	16.4	7.7	33.2	17.6	15.9	16.8
S&P 500 INDEX- BUY & HOLD		30.4	-3.1	31.7	16.5	5.2	12.4	15.3	13.9

NOTES:
1. PERFORMANCE RESULTS ARE BASED UPON THE ANNUAL RETURNS PUBLISHED IN THE JANUARY 1992 ISSUE OF THE HULBERT FINANCIAL DIGEST. THE TIMING MODELS SHOWN HAVE AT LEAST FIVE YEARS OF PERFORMANCE DATA; ALSO, THESE MODELS SWITCH TO CASH WHEN A SELL SIGNAL IS GENERATED.
2. LPR = LONG-TERM PERFORMANCE RATING = MEAN (OR GEOMETRIC AVERAGE) OF THE 2-YR MAR AND 5-YR MAR.
3. AS SHOWN IN TABLES 24A/B, SYSTEMS & FORECASTS AND INVESTOR INTELLIGENCE WERE THE TWO TOP-PERFORMING MKTIME NEWSLETTERS WHEN TIMING THE WILSHIRE 5000 INDEX DURING THE 5-YEAR PERIOD. WHEN TIMING THE S&P 500 INDEX, INVESTORS INTELLIGENCE OUTPERFORMED SYSTEMS & FORECASTS WITH AND WITHOUT ADJUSTMENT FOR MUTUAL FUND TRADING FEES. THE PERFORMANCE DATA FOR THE S&P 500 INDEX WHEN TIMED BY THESE NEWSLETTERS WAS COMPUTED USING THEIR BUY/SELL SIGNALS.

Forecasts and *Investors Intelligence Newsletters* during the 5-year period. Using these signal dates, we computed the LPR values (adjusted for mutual fund trading fees) for the S&P 500 Index when timed by the two newsletters. The LPR values are as follows:

Investors Intelligence	16.8%
Systems & Forecasts	14.7%

We therefore selected the *Investors Intelligence Newsletter* as the top-performing 1992 mktime newsletter.

Table 24C provides the 5-year performance data for the S&P 500 Index when timed by the Investors Intelligence newsletter and when bought and held.

Table 25 provides a directory for three of the four mktime newsletters that outperformed Buy/Hold when timing the Wilshire 5000 Index. When bought and held, the Wilshire 5000 Index had a 5-year LPR of 13.3%

Audited Market Timers

The MoniResearch Corporation tracks the past performance of professional money managers who employ market timing. The corporation reports the results in the *MoniResearch Newsletter*. Thus, MoniResearch Corporation is providing an objective, quantitative evaluation of the performance of professional market timers in the same manner as *Hulbert Financial Digest* does for stock and mutual fund newsletters. However, MoniResearch only reports on market timers who are managing customer accounts as distinct from newsletters. The data presented below is based upon performance results shown in the March/April 1992 issue of the newsletter.

MoniResearch Performance Evaluation Procedure

At the present time, the *MoniResearch Newsletter* reports on the performance of over 40 professional market timers. There are many more market timers in the U.S., but for obvious reasons, only the better performers are interested in publicizing their results. MoniResearch classifies these 40 market timers in two

TABLE 25
DIRECTORY OF 1992 TOP-PERFORMING MKTIME NEWSLETTERS (1) TRACKED BY HULBERT FINANCIAL DIGEST

RANK BY LPR	NEWSLETTER	LPR (%) (2/3)	NEWSLETTER ADDRESS	NEWSLETTER EDITOR/ PHONE #	ANNUAL FEE
1	INVESTORS INTELLIGENCE (FOR SWITCH FUND TRADERS)	17.5	P.O. BOX 2046 NEW ROCHELLE, NY 10801	MICHAEL BURKE 914-632-0422	$124
2	GRANVILLE MARKET LETTER	16.0	P.O. DRAWER 413006 KANSAS CITY, MO 64141	JOE GRANVILLE 816-474-5353	$250
3	SYSTEMS & FORECASTS	15.9	150 GREAT NECK RD. GREAT NECK, NY 11021	GERALD APPEL 516-829-6444	$175

NOTES:

1. SEE TABLES 24/A/B.
2. LPR = LONG-TERM PERFORMANCE RATING = MEAN (OR GEOMETRIC AVERAGE) OF THE 2-YEAR MAR AND 5-YEAR MAR.
3. THE LPR VALUE SHOWN IS FOR THE WILSHIRE 5000 INDEX WHEN TIMED. IT HAS BEEN ADJUSTED FOR MUTUAL FUND TRADING FEES.

groups (either "A" or "B" group). The criteria for acceptance in each group are described below.

To be accepted into the "A" group, a market timer must meet **all the** following criteria:

- Managed client accounts for a minimum of five years.
- Assets under management of at least $20 million.
- Provide a continuous record of customer statements for the period under study. This data is used by *MoniResearch* to *validate* the Buy/Sell historical signals claimed by a market timer.

Bona fide market timers who meet "A" group criteria (3) but not criteria (1) and/or (2) are accepted into *MoniResearch's* "B" group. Some market timers do not have five years experience in managing client accounts. In such cases, hypothetical Buy/Sell signals are accepted for the initial period. Such hypothetical signals are either:

- Signals that were actually generated at the time but customer statements (to validate such signals) are not available, or
- Signals that would have been generated if their present market timing model had been used.

MoniResearch computes and reports upon the performance of "A" and "B" group market timers using the Buy/Sell history derived from the market timer's customer statements. Annualized rates of return are computed for one, three and five years for investments made in the S&P 500 Index as described below. *MoniResearch* computes market timer annualized returns as follows:

- When a Buy signal occurs, account assets are switched into the S&P 500 Index adjusted for dividends, distributions and splits.
- When a Sell signal occurs, account assets are switched into a hypothetical money market account that has a yield equal to the 3-month T-bill plus 0.25%.
- At the end of each year, a management fee (approximately 2% or less, depending upon an account's market value) is deducted from the account.

- Each issue of the MoniResearch Newsletter contains performance results for the market timers in either "A" or "B" group.

Determining the 1992 Top-Performing Audited Market Timers

Tables 26A and 26B provide the following performance data for the S&P 500 Index when timed by the 21 "A" group market timers listed in the March/April 1992 issue of the *MoniResearch Newsletter:*

1. Annual Returns
2. 2-year and 5-year mean annualized returns (MARs) or compounded rates of return
3. Long-term performance rating (LPR) which equals the mean (or geometric average) of the 2-year MAR and 5-year MAR.

Table 26A shows performance results that have **not** been adjusted for mutual fund trading fees. In the table, the market timers are ranked by their LPR values.

Table 26B shows performance results (for the three top-performing market timers indicated in table 26A) that have been adjusted for mutual fund trading fees where applicable. This table indicates that Lincoln Investment Planning (with an LPR of 16.3%) is the top-performing 1992 audited market timer.

Table 26A also indicates that:

- Three market timers outperformed the S&P 500 Index when bought and held.
- Seven market timers had LPR values less than money market funds, when bought and held.

Table 27 provides a directory of the three top-performing, audited market timers during the preceding five years.

The Five 1992 Top-Performing Mktime Models

In the preceding paragraphs, we evaluated the performance during the previous five years (1987 to 1991) of 45 candidate mktime models. The performance data was available from three sources as indicated in Table 28. This table also indicates that, as described above, we made an initial screening and selected seven (7) mktime models for further consideration. In the following paragraph, we perform the final screening and select the five (5) top-performing mktime models for use during 1992.

TABLE 26A

PERFORMANCE RESULTS WITHOUT ADJUSTMENT FOR TRADING FEES FOR S&P 500 INDEX TIMED BY MARKET TIMERS AUDITED BY MONIRESEARCH NEWSLETTER: 5-YR PERIOD FROM 1987 TO 1991

LPR		ANNUAL RETURNS (%)					MAR (%)		
RANK	**AUDITED MARKET TIMERS**	**1991**	**1990**	**1989**	**1988**	**1987**	**2-YR**	**5-YR**	**LPR (%)**
1	LINCOLN INVESTMENT PLANNING	25.3	6.9	15.3	8.6	29.9	15.7	16.9	16.3
2	FLEXIBLE PLAN INVESTMENT, LTD	25.4	4.5	18.0	12.4	24.8	14.5	16.7	15.6
3	MEEDER (R.) & ASSOCIATES	23.0	7.3	17.9	9.3	21.8	14.9	15.7	15.3
	BUY/HOLD S&P 500 INDEX	30.4	-3.1	31.7	16.5	5.2	12.4	15.3	13.9
4	FINANCIAL SERVICES ADVISORY	14.7	4.1	23.4	3.9	32.4	9.3	15.2	12.2
5	HAMPTON INVESTORS, INC.	21.8	3.1	16.8	-1.9	21.7	12.1	11.9	12.0
6	LEARY (R.M.) & CO.	15.1	0.0	26.5	7.2	20.8	7.3	13.5	10.4
7	ZWEIG/AVATAR	18.4	-1.9	16.1	4.9	27.5	7.8	12.5	10.1
8	AFC ADVISORY SERVICES	16.2	0.0	6.7	5.0	31.5	7.8	11.4	9.6
9	SCHABACKER INVEST. MGMT.	19.5	-0.9	18.4	10.1	5.5	8.8	10.2	9.5
10	SCHIELD MGMT CO.	20.1	1.2	2.2	0.8	21.6	10.2	8.8	9.5
11	LOWRY MGMT CORP.	14.5	-1.3	17.9	10.4	20.9	6.3	12.2	9.2
12	VARI INVESTOR SERVICES	18.9	-4.8	29.8	-3.3	19.6	6.4	11.2	8.8
13	MARKETARIAN, INC.	25.2	-7.9	11.3	1.4	24.1	7.4	10.1	8.7
14	MERRIMAN (PAUL A.) & ASSOC.	13.6	0.9	11.7	1.8	18.3	7.1	9.0	8.0
	BUY/HOLD MONEY MARKET	6.1	8.0	8.7	7.0	6.2	7.0	7.2	7.1
15	MONITREND ASSETS MGMT CORP.	11.0	5.4	9.3	4.9	-1.0	8.2	5.8	7.0
16	KOYEN & ASSOCIATES	6.2	3.6	24.0	0.0	13.3	4.9	9.1	7.0
17	PORTFOLIO TIMING INC.	17.4	-3.8	1.8	3.3	20.4	6.3	7.4	6.8
18	TRENDSTAT CAPITAL MGMT	2.7	-0.7	25.7	4.0	21.5	1.0	10.1	5.5
19	KIRKLAND INVESTMENT MGMT	2.9	1.5	19.1	2.5	20.7	2.2	9.0	5.5
20	BERER (SHOAL P) ASSOC, INC.	5.3	4.1	15.8	4.8	2.7	4.7	6.4	5.5
21	NATIONAL INVESTMENT ADVISORS	3.1	-5.1	8.8	7.7	7.2	-1.1	4.2	1.5

TABLE 26B
PERFORMANCE RESULTS ADJUSTED FOR MUTUAL FUND TRADING FEES FOR S&P 500 INDEX WHEN TIMED BY THE TOP THREE 1992 MARKET TIMERS AUDITED BY MONIRESEARCH NEWSLETTER: DURING 5-YEAR PERIOD FROM 1987 TO 1991

		ANNUAL RETURNS (%)					MAR (%)		
RANK BY LPR	AUDITED MARKET TIMERS	1991	1990	1989	1988	1987	2-YR MAR	5-YR MAR	LPR (%) (3)
1	LINCOLN INVESTMENT PLANNING	25.3	6.9	15.3	8.6	29.9	15.7	16.9	16.3
2	FLEXIBLE PLAN INVESTMENT, LTD	25.4	4.5	18.0	12.4	24.8	14.5	16.7	15.6
3	MEEDER & ASSOC. (2)	21.3	5.6	16.2	7.6	20.1	14.0	13.2	13.6
	BUY/HOLD S&P 500 INDEX	30.4	-3.1	31.7	16.5	5.2	12.4	15.3	13.9

NOTES:

1. PERFORMANCE RESULTS WERE COMPUTED FROM DATA PROVIDED BY THE MONIRESEARCH NEWSLETTER, P.O. BOX 19146, PORTLAND, OR 97219
2. ANNUAL RETURNS HAVE BEEN ADJUSTED FOR MUTUAL FUND TRADING FEES BY 0.17% TIMES THE AVERAGE NUMBER OF SWITCHES PER YEAR.
3. LPR (LONG-TERM PERFORMANCE RATING) EQUALS THE MEAN (OR GEOMETRIC AVERAGE) OF THE 2-YEAR AND 5-YEAR MEAN ANNUALIZED RETURNS.

TABLE 27
DIRECTORY : THE THREE 1992 TOP-PERFORMING MARKET TIMERS AUDITED BY MONIRESEARCH NEWSLETTER: 5-YEAR PERIOD FROM 1987 TO 1991

RANK BY LPR	AUDITED MARKET TIMER NAME/ADDRESS	PHONE #	AVG # SWITCHES PER YR	VOLATILITY	ANNUAL FEE
1	LINCOLN INVESTMENT PLANNING THE FORST PAVILLION, STE. 2000 WYNCOTE, PA 19095	(215) 887-8111 (800) 242-1421	3.6	0.43	2.3% 1ST $100,000 1.8% NEXT $400,000
2	FLEXIBLE PLAN INVESTMENT, LTD. 3883 TELEGRAPH BLOOMFIELD HILLS, MI 48013	(313) 642-6640	4.8	0.39	2.8% 1ST $50,000 SUBTRACT 0.1% FOR EACH $50,000 THEREAFTER UNTIL REACHING 0.9%
3	MEEDER & ASSOCIATES 6000 MEMORIAL DRIVE DUBLIN, OH 43017	(800) 325-3539	10.0	0.44	1.5% EXPENSE RATIO FOR MUIRFIELD FUND

TABLE 28
RESULTS OF SCREENING PROCESS TO DETERMINE THE 1992 TOP-PERFORMING MARKET TIMING MODELS

MKTIME MODEL CATEGORY & INDEPENDENT PERFORMANCE EVALUATOR	# CANDIDATES	NUMBER SELECTED	
		INTIAL SCREENING	FINAL SCREENING
MKTIME MODELS DEVELOPED AND/OR EVALUATED BY ASSN. OF MUTUAL FUND INVESTORS (AMFI)	5	5	4
MARKET TIMING NEWSLETTERS TRACKED BY THE HULBERT FINANCIAL DIGEST	19	1	1
PROFESSIONAL MARKET TIMERS AUDITED BY THE MONIRESEARCH CORPORATION	21	1	0
TOTAL	45	7	5

Table 29 indicates the performance results during the previous five years for the seven top-performing mktime models. The models are ranked by their LPR values. *The table indicates that four AMFI mktime models (MTM2,3,5 and 6) and the top-performing mktime newsletter (Investors Intelligence) had the five highest LPR values. We therefore selected these five mktime models as the five 1992 top-performers.* Table 30 lists and briefly describes these five top-performing mktime models. Figure 9 graphically illustrates the LPR and 5-year MAR for each of the five 1992 top-performing mktime models.

Table 31 indicates that the MTM6-timed S&P 500 Index fund outperformed the index when bought and held during the 5-year period by the following significant margins:

5-Year MAR:	27.1% vs 15.4%
Inflation-Adjusted 5-Year Total Return:	160% vs 60%
Inflation-Adjusted Future Value of a $1,000 Lump Sum Investment:	$2,600 vs. $1,600

The 1993 Top-Performing Mktime Models

As indicated in Table 21, the only 1993 mktime model performance data available at this time (January 1993) is data for the five AMFI mktime models. Since at least four of those mktime models have been selected as top-performers during the past three years, we have made a preliminary selection of the AMFI mktime models as the five 1993 top-performing mktime models. Table 23B presents the performance data for the five AMFI mktime models during the 5-year period preceding 1993; namely, 1988 through 1992.

TABLE 29
PERFORMANCE RESULTS FOR S&P 500 INDEX WHEN TIMED BY THE SEVEN (7) 1992 TOP-PERFORMING MKTIME MODELS DURING 5-YEAR PERIOD FROM 1987 TO 1991

LPR RANK	MARKET TIMING MODEL (SEE NOTE 1)	NET ANNUAL RETURNS (%) 1991	1990	1989	1988	1987	5-YR MAR (2)	2-YR MAR (2)	LPR (%) (3)
1	MTM6 (MTM5 + MTM4) *	33.5	11.7	32.6	22.0	37.6	27.1	22.1	24.6
2	MTM5 (AIQ SOFTWARE)*	30.7	11.2	27.4	13.8	26.5	21.7	20.6	21.1
3	MTM3 (MVG AVERAGES PLUS)	28.9	-0.4	30.6	16.4	33.1	21.0	13.3	17.1
4	MTM2 (S&P 500 DVD YLD)	30.5	-3.1	31.7	16.6	36.0	21.4	12.5	16.9
5	MTMX (INVESTORS INTELLIGENCE-#1 MKTIME NEWSLTR)	23.8	8.6	16.4	7.7	33.2	17.6	15.9	16.8
6	MTMY (LINCOLN INVESTMENT PLANNING -#1 AUDITED MARKET TIMER)	25.3	6.9	15.3	8.6	29.9	15.7	16.9	16.3
7	MTM4 (SEASONALITY)*	7.4	16.6	19.3	24.7	22.3	17.9	11.9	14.9
	MTMI (BUY/HOLD)	30.5	-3.1	31.7	16.6	5.2	15.4	12.5	13.9

NOTES:

1. SEE TABLE 22 FOR DESCRIPTION OF THE AMFI MKTIME MODELS (MTM2 TO MTM6).
2. MAR = MEAN ANNUALIZED RETURN OR COMPOUNDED RATE OF RETURN.
3. LPR = LONG-TERM PERFORMANCE RATING = MEAN (OR GEOMETRIC AVERAGE) OF 5-YR MAR AND 2-YR MAR.
4. * INDICATES THAT THE ANNUAL RETURNS HAVE BEEN ADJUSTED FOR MUTUAL FUND TRADING FEES.

TABLE 30
THE FIVE 1992 TOP-PERFORMING MARKET TIMING MODELS: COMPARATI VE CHARACTERISTICS

RANK BY LPR	MKTIME MODEL ID	MKTIME MODEL DESCRIPTION	DATA INPUT FREQUENCY	AVG # SWITCHES PER YR.	S&P 500 INDEX TIMED DURING 5-YR PERIOD ENDING 12/31/91: 5-YR MAR (NOTE 1)	5-YR LPR (NOTE 2)
1	MTM6	THIS MODEL COMBINES MODIFIED VERSIONS OF THE MTM4 AND MTM5 MKTIME MODELS. THE MODIFICATIONS ARE DETERMINED BY COMPUTER BACK-TESTING OVER PERIODS FROM 5 TO 12 YEARS (SEE APPENDIX F).	DAILY	12	27.1	24.6
2	MTM5	AIQ MARKETEXPERT SOFTWARE SYSTEM, VERSION 3.5.1. THIS SYSTEM EMPLOYS ABOUT 25 MKTIME INDICATORS WHICH ARE WEIGHTED TO GENERATE BUY OR SELL SIGNALS. AIQ SYSTEMS, INC. (800-332-2999) AND IS EXECUTED ON A PC (SEE APPENDIX E).	DAILY	10	21.7	21.1
3	MTM3	FOUR MKTIME INDICATORS ARE EMPLOYED TO GENERATE BUY OR SELL SIGNALS. THE INDICATORS INCLUDE THE S&P 500 DIVIDEND YIELD AND TWO 39-WEEK MOVING AVERAGES (SEE APPENDIX C).	WEEKLY	2	21	17.1
4	MTM2	S&P 500 DIVIDEND YIELD IS EMPLOYED AS THE SOLE MKTIME INDICATOR (SEE APPENDIX B).	WEEKLY	0.4	21.4	16.9
5	MTMX	INVESTORS INTELLIGENCE NEWSLETTER P.O. BOX 2046, NEW ROCHELLE, NY 10801 (914) 632-0422.	DAILY	13	15.9	16.8
	MTM1	S&P 500 INDEX WHEN BOUGHT AND HELD	NA	-0-	15.4	13.9

NOTES:
1. MAR = MEAN ANNUALIZED RETURN OR COMPOUNDED RATE OF RETURN.
2. LPR = LONG-TERM PERFORMANCE RATING = MEAN (OR GEOMETRIC AVERAGE) OF THE 5-YR MAR AND 2-YR MAR.
3. ANNUALIZED AND ANNUAL RETURNS HAVE BEEN ADJUSTED FOR MUTUAL FUND TRADING FEES.

FIGURE 9

87-91 RETURNS OF S&P 500 INDEX WHEN
TIMED BY 1992 TOP MKTIME MODELS
5-YR MAR (%) OR 5-YR LPR (%)
30
25
20
15
10
5
0
MTM6
MTM5
MTM3
MTM2
MTMX
B&H
1992 TOP-PERFORMING MKTIME MODELS & B&H
5-YR LPR
5-YR MAR

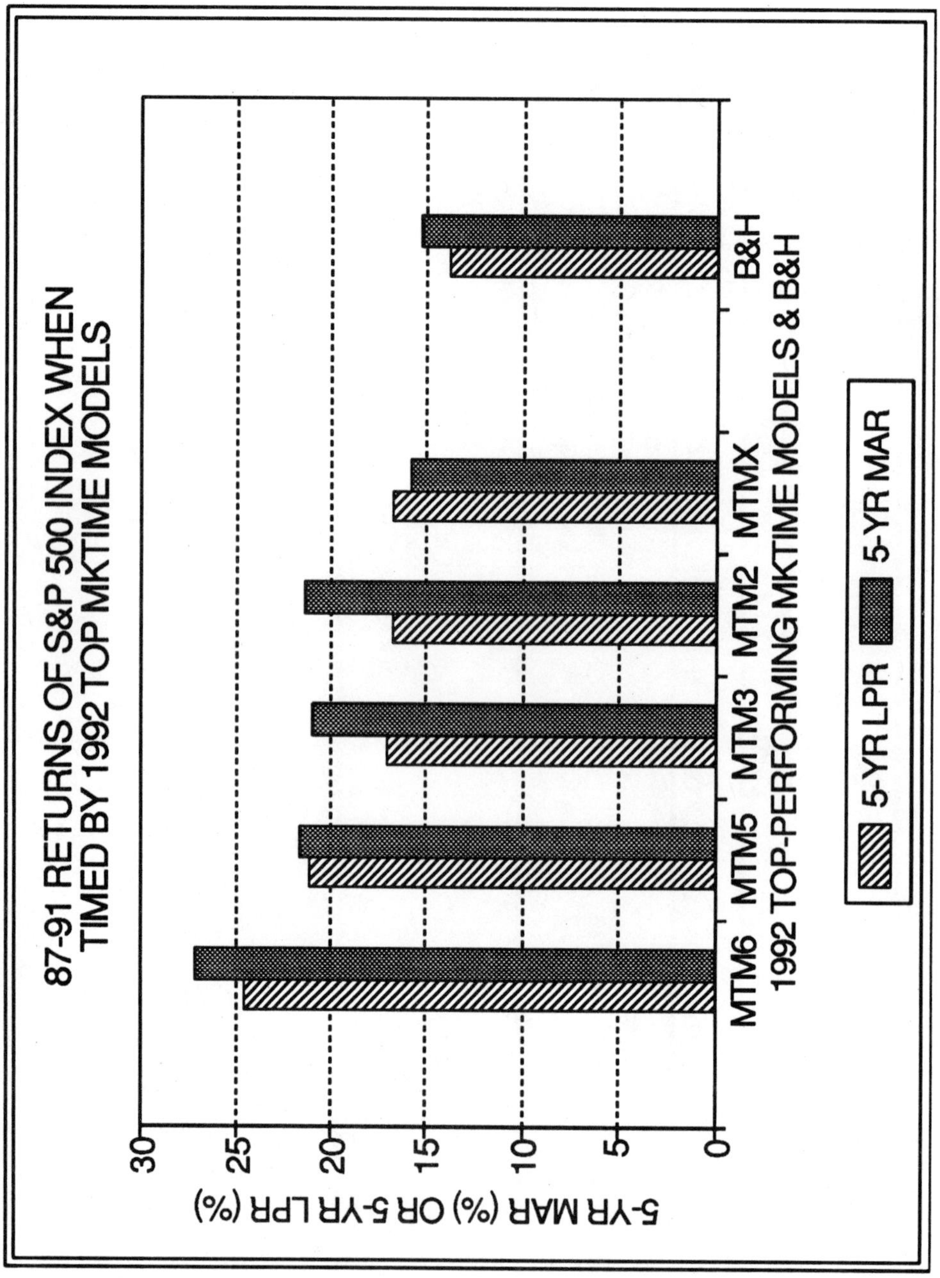

TABLE 31
HYPOTHETICAL INVESTMENT PERFORMANCE OF S&P 500 INDEX FUND WHEN TIMED BY THE 1992 TOP-PERFORMING MKTIME MODEL (MTM6) DURING THE 5-YEAR PERIOD FROM 1987 TO 1991

PHASE	DESCRIPTION	MEAN ANNUALIZED RETURN (%)	INFLATION-ADJUSTED @ 5%/YR	
			TOTAL 5-YEAR RETURN	FUTURE VALUE (NOTE 1)
I	S&P 500 INDEX BOUGHT & HELD	15.4	60%	$1,600
II	S&P 500 INDEX WHEN MTM6-TIMED	27.1	160%	$2,600

NOTES:
1. FUTURE VALUE ON 12/31/91 IS BASED UPON A LUMP SUM INVESTMENT OF $1,000 ON 12/31/86

5: GROWTH FUND SELECTION SYSTEMS

Introduction

In paragraph Chapter 3 and Table 18A, we discussed how our mutual fund investment strategy has evolved during the 7-year period from 1986 through 1992. Thus far, we have described Phases I and II of this strategy.

In Phase I, we bought and held an index fund that invests in the 500 stocks comprising the S&P 500 Index. In Phase II, we used the top-performing mktime model to determine when we should be invested in the index fund and when we should be invested in the money market fund. With the Phase I strategy, we would have achieved a MAR of **16.7%** during the 11-year period from 1982 through 1992. Using the Phase II strategy, we would have increased our MAR during the 11-year period to **23.2%**. In Phase III, we employ a growth fund selection system (GFSS) to determine which growth or index fund should be our investment vehicle when the mktime model generates a Buy signal. Using the Phase III investment strategy, we would have increased our 11-year MAR to **38.3%**. (See Chapter 7).

In this section, we describe the GFSS2 growth fund selection system which is used with mktime models MTM4, MTM5 and MTM6. The GFSS2 selection system was developed and tested during 1992 as an improved version of the GFSS1 predecessor selection system. To date, no effective growth fund selection system has been developed for use with mktime models MTM1, MTM2 and MTM3.

How the GFSS2 Selection System Works

Table 32 briefly outlines the step-by-step procedure used by the GFSS2 growth fund selection system.

- Step 1 involves the determination (at the start of each year) of the high-volatility, no-load growth funds. These funds have volatilities equal to or greater than the volatility of the S&P 500 Index.

TABLE 32
GFSS2 GROWTH FUND SELECTION SYSTEM
FUND SELECTION PROCEDURE FOR USE WITH A SPECIFIC MKTIME MODEL

STEP #	WHEN PERFORMED	STEP DESCRIPTION
1	AT THE START OF EACH YEAR	DETERMINE THE HIGH-VOLATILITY, NO-LOAD GROWTH (STOCK) FUNDS WITH VOLATILITIES ABOVE 1.0 (USUALLY 10 TO 25 FUNDS).
2	AT THE START OF EACH YEAR	DETERMINE THE FIVE TOP-PERFORMING, HIGH-VOLATILITY GROWTH FUNDS WHEN TIMED BY THE MKTIME MODEL DURING THE PREVIOUS FIVE YEARS.
3	WHEN A BUY SIGNAL IS GENERATED DURING THE YEAR	DETERMINE THE TOP-PERFORMING MAJOR MARKET INDEX (OTCI, S&P 500 OR DJIA) DURING THE PREVIOUS 13 DAYS. IF THE OTCI IS THE TOP PERFORMER, INVEST IN THE GROWTH FUNDS SELECTED IN STEP 2; OTHERWISE, INVEST IN THE TOP-PERFORMING INDEX FUND.

NOTES:

1. THE GFSSI SELECTION SYSTEM EMPLOYS ONLY STEPS 1 AND 2.
2. OTCI = OVER-THE-COUNTER INDUSTRIAL
3. DJIA = DOW-JONES INDUSTRIAL AVERAGE

- Step 2 is also performed at the start of each year. All the high-volatility growth funds are timed by each of the applicable mktime models during the previous five years. The 5-year LPR value is computed for each growth fund. Then, the funds are ranked by their LPR value. The five funds with the highest LPR values are selected for use as investment vehicles (with the applicable mktime model) during the year in the manner described below.

  The high-volatility growth funds selected in Step 2 are highly correlated with the OTCI (Over-the-Counter-Industrial) Index. The OTCI, S&P 500 and DJIA (Dow Jones Industrial Average) indices are also highly correlated with each other. However, during certain periods such as in 1984 and 1992, these indices have moved in opposite directions. During such periods, the GFSS1 predecessor selection system incurred significant losses. In order to minimize such losses, Step 3 was added in the GFSS2 selection system.

- In Step 3, we determine which of the three indices is the top performer during the 13 days preceding a Buy signal. If the OTCI Index is the top performer when a Buy signal is generated, we invest in the growth funds selected in Step 2. If the S&P 500 Index is the top performer, we invest in the Federated Max Cap fund. This fund is a no-load index fund that invests in the S&P 500 stocks and that permits frequent asset switching via a mutual fund trading broker. If the DJIA is the top performer, we invest in the ASM fund. This fund is an index fund that invests in the 30 DJIA stocks and that permits frequent asset switching.

GFSS2 Index-Selection Indicators and Rules

Table 33A describes the four indicators used in Step 3 to select the top-performing market index each day. These indicators measure the difference in performance during the preceding 13 days between (1) OTCI and S&P 500 indices and (2) OTCI and the DJIA indices. These indicators have been designated as:

SP DIFF **SP DIFF Moving Average**

DJ DIFF **DJ DIFF Moving Average**

Table 33B defines the rules used to select the top-performing market index. The OTCI Index is selected as the top performer if at least one of the above four indicators is positive. The OTCI

TABLE 33A
GFSS2 GROWTH FUND SELECTION SYSTEM
MAJOR-MARKET-INDEX SELECTION INDICATORS

1. SP/4D = DIFFERENCE BETWEEN THE 4-DAY RETURNS OF THE OTCI AND S&P 500 INDICES
2. SP/9D = DIFFERENCE BETWEEN THE 9-DAY RETURNS OF THE OTCI AND S&P 500 INDICES
3. SP DIFF IS THE AVERAGE OF THE SP/4D AND SP/9D VALUES*

4. DJ/4D = DIFFERENCE BETWEEN THE 4-DAY RETURNS OF THE OTCI AND DJIA INDICES
5. DJ/9D = DIFFERENCE BETWEEN THE 9-DAY RETURNS OF THE OTCI AND DJIA INDICES
6. DJ DIFF IS THE AVERAGE OF THE DJ/4D AND DJ/9D VALUES*

7. SP DIFF MVG AVG IS THE 5-DAY MOVING AVERAGE OF THE SP DIFF*
8. DJ DIFF MVG AVG IS THE 5-DAY MOVING AVERAGE OF THE DJ DIFF*

NOTES:
1. DJIA = DOW-JONES INDUSTRIAL AVERAGE
2. OTCI = OVER-THE-COUNTER INDUSTRIAL
3. * THESE FOUR INDICATORS ARE USED TO SELECT THE TOP-PERFORMING MAJOR MARKET INDEX (OTCI,S&P 500 OR DJIA) WHEN A BUY SIGNAL IS GENERATED.

TABLE 33B
GFSS2 GROWTH FUND SELECTION SYSTEM
MAJOR-MARKET-INDEX SELECTION RULES

1. INVEST IN A S&P 500 INDEX FUND OR DJIA INDEX FUND IF ALL OF THE FOLLOWING INDICATORS ARE NEGATIVE WHEN A BUY SIGNAL IS GENERATED:

SP DIFF DJ DIFF SP DIFF MVG AVG DJ DIFF MVG AVG

OTHERWISE, INVEST IN ONE OR MORE OF THE FIVE TOP-PERFORMING, HIGH-VOLATILITY, NO-LOAD GROWTH FUNDS SELECTED FOR THE CURRENT YEAR.

2. IF ALL OF THE ABOVE INDICATORS ARE NEGATIVE WHEN A BUY SIGNAL IS GENERATED, INVEST IN THE INDEX FUND WITH GREATEST DIFFERENCE BETWEEN ITS DIFF VALUE AND ITS DIFF 5-DAY MOVING AVERAGE.

3. INDICATORS BETWEEN -0.09 AND +0.09 ARE NOT COUNTED.

Index is **not** selected if all four of the above indicators is negative. Instead, one of the index funds (S&P or DJIA) is selected for investment. The index fund with the greatest difference between its DIFF value and its DIFF 5-day moving average is selected.

How GFSS2 Selection Worked in 1989

The following paragraphs illustrate how the GFSS2 growth fund selection system worked in 1989 in conjunction with the MTM6 mktime model.

The first step in selecting a growth fund for investment is illustrated in Table 34. This table lists the high-volatility, no-load diversified growth funds during the five years preceding 1989. These funds were the initial 1989 growth fund candidates.

The second step in selecting a growth fund for investment is to determine which of the *initial* growth fund candidates are the five top performers when timed. This determination is based upon the timed performance of the growth fund candidates during the previous five years; i.e., 1984 to 1988 in this case.

Table 35 illustrates the computation of the 5-year LPR (long-term performance rating) for each of the 10 initial 1989 candidates when timed by the MTM6 mktime model. Table 35 lists the growth funds by their LPR values. It shows that 20th Century Vista fund was the top fund for 1989 investment with an LPR value of 42.7%.

The third step in selecting a growth fund for investment is to determine which of the major market indices is the top performer when a Buy signal is generated during the year. Table 36 illustrates the index selection process during 1989. The table shows how a market index was selected for each Buy/Sell transaction. A Buy/Sell transaction begins when a Buy signal is executed and ends when the next Buy signal is executed. The transaction includes one Buy cycle (investment in a growth fund) and one Sell cycle (investment in a money market fund).

Table 36A indicates that there were eight Buy/Sell transactions during 1989. The OTCI Index was selected for four transactions and the S&P 500 Index was selected for the other four transactions. Note that the S&P 500 Index was selected for transaction #89-6 because the SP DIFF value of 0.01 was too small to be counted.

TABLE 34
GFSS GROWTH FUND SELECTION PROCEDURE
STEP 1: DETERMINE HIGH-VOLATILITY, NO-LOAD GROWTH FUND CANDIDATES (1) FOR 1989 INVESTMENT

RANK BY VOLATILITY	GROWTH FUND	VOLATILITY
1	20TH CENTURY VISTA	1.34
2	20TH CENTURY ULTRA	1.31
3	20TH CENTURY GROWTH	1.20
4	20TH CENTURY SELECT	1.10
5	STEINROE STOCK	1.07
6	STEINROE CAPITAL OPPORTUNITY	1.07
7	TUDOR	1.06
8	FINANCIAL DYNAMICS	1.06
9	NEUBERGER MANHATTAN	1.04
10	VL SPECIAL SITUATIONS	1.00
	S&P 500 INDEX	1.00

NOTES:

1. THE GROWTH FUND CANDIDATES ARE THOSE NO-LOAD FUNDS WITH VOLATILITIES OF 1.0 OR GREATER AND WITH PERFROMANCE DATA AVAILABLE FOR THE PREVIOUS FIVE YEARS.

TABLE 35
GROWTH FUND SELECTION SYSTEMS GFSS1 & GFSS2 (1)
STEP 2: ANNUAL SELECTION OF THE FIVE TOP-PERFORMING GROWTH FUNDS (2) FOR 1989 INVESTMENT USING THE MTM6 MKTIME MODEL

		MTM6-TIMED ANNUAL RETURNS (%)					PERFORMANCE ELEMENTS (3)		
RANK BY LPR	**GROWTH FUND**	**1988**	**1987**	**1986**	**1985**	**1984**	**5MAR**	**2MAR**	**LPR**
1	20TH CENTURY VISTA	32.7	77.5	45.0	26.3	-4.4	32.7	53.5	42.7
2	20TH CENTURY ULTRA	37.2	67.0	30.1	26.2	-7.9	28.2	51.3	39.3
3	FINANCIAL DYNAMICS	32.4	67.9	23.0	29.4	-1.2	28.4	49.1	38.4
4	TUDOR	29.7	57.4	25.4	25.9	2.5	27.0	42.9	34.7
5	NEUBERGER MANHATTAN	29.1	44.8	32.8	37.1	15.1	31.4	36.7	34.0
6	STEINROE CAPTL OPPORTUNITY	22.1	64.8	27.7	25.2	-5.5	24.9	41.8	33.1
7	20TH CENTURY GROWTH	14.8	54.5	32.3	35.9	-4.8	24.9	33.2	29.0
8	VL SPECIAL SITUATIONS	24.7	44.8	23.2	28.3	-12.6	20.1	34.4	27.0
9	20TH CENTURY SELECT	18.5	39.7	34.0	34.4	0.8	24.6	28.7	26.6
10	STEINROE STOCK	12.6	50.8	28.1	28.2	-4.0	21.8	30.3	26.0

NOTES:

1. SEE TABLE 32 FOR A BRIEF DESCRIPTION OF THE GFSSI AND GFSS2 GROWTH FUND SELECTION SYSTEMS.
2. THE FIVE TOP-PERFORMING GROWTH FUNDS FOR EACH YEAR ARE SELECTED ON THE BASIS OF THEIR TIMED PERFORMANCE DURING THE PREVIOUS FIVE YEARS. THE CANDIDATE FUNDS LISTED IN TABLE 34 ARE RANKED BY THEIR LPR (LONG-TERM PERFORMANCE) VALUES IN ORDER TO MAKE THE SELECTION.
3. MAR = MEAN ANNUALIZED RETURN OR COMPOUNDED RATE OF RETURN OVER A PERIOD OF YEARS. 5MAR = 5-YEAR MAR; 2MAR = 2-YEAR MAR
LPR = MEAN (OR GEOMETRIC AVERAGE) OF THE 5MAR AND 2MAR

TABLE 36
COMPUTATION OF 1989 NET ANNUAL RETURN FOR GFSS2-SELECTED GROWTH FUNDS WHEN TIMED BY MTM6 MKTIME MODEL

A. INDEX SELECTION INDICATORS FOR EACH BUY/SELL TRANSACTION

INDEX SELECTION INDICATOR (SEE TABLE 33A)	BUY/SELL TRANSACTION NUMBERS							
	#88-6B FM 1/01 TO 3/29	#89-1 FM 3/29 TO 6/29	#89-2 FM 6/29 TO 7/11	#89-3 FM 7/11 TO 8/30	#89-4 FM 8/30 TO 9/28	#89-5 FM 9/28 TO 10/30	#89-6 FM 10/30 TO 12/27	#89-7A FM 12/27 TO 12/29
SP DIFF	0.86	0.14	-2.01	-0.97	-0.15	-0.15	0.01	1.30
DJ DIFF	0.46	0.05	-1.63	-0.51	-0.32	0.03	-0.16	1.76
SP DIFF MOVING AVERAGE	0.64	0.02	-1.63	-0.90	-0.30	0.08	-0.43	-0.13
DJ DIFF MOVING AVERAGE	0.08	0.34	-1.43	-0.51	-0.34	0.36	-0.40	0.03
SELECTED INDEX (TABLE 33B)	OTCI	OTCI	SP	SP	SP	OTCI	SP	OTCI

B. BUY/SELL TRANSACTION RETURNS FOR SELECTED INDEX OR GROWTH FUND

INDEX OR TOP-PERFORMING NO-LOAD GROWTH FUND FOR 1989 INVESTMENT	BUY/SELL GROSS TRANSACTION RETURNS								NET ANNUAL RETURN ADJUSTED FOR TRADING FEES
	#88-6B FM 1/01 TO 3/29	#89-1 FM 3/29 TO 6/29	#89-2 FM 6/29 TO 7/11	#89-3 FM 7/11 TO 8/30	#89-4 FM 8/30 TO 9/28	#89-5 FM 9/28 TO 10/30	#89-6 FM 10/30 TO 12/27	#89-7A FM 12/27 TO 12/29	
S&P 500 INDEX	5.4	12.0	1.8	5.1	-0.1	2.4	3.2	1.3	
GFSS1-SELECTED TOP FUND *	10.0	18.2	4.5	0.4	0.2	4.3	-2.0	2.4	40.7
GFSS2-SELECTED TOP FUND	10.0	18.2	1.8	5.1	-0.1	4.3	3.2	2.4	50.7

* 20TH CENTURY VISTA DURING 1989

Table 36B indicates the 1989 transaction returns for (1) the S&P 500 Index; (2) the GFSS1-selected top fund; and (3) the GFSS2-selected top fund. GFSS1 is the previous growth fund selection system which did not employ index selection as a prelude to growth fund selection. Therefore, the top growth fund selected in Step 2 is always selected for investment when a Buy signal is generated. Table 36B shows that the GFSS2-selected fund achieved a net annual return of 50.7% as compared with 40.7% for the GFSS1-selected fund (20th Century Vista fund).

How GFSS2 Step 3 Worked in 1984 and 1992

Table 37A illustrates market index selection for 1984 when only the S&P 500 Index was considered. The table shows that all four index selection indicators were negative for each of the three 1984 Buy/Sell transactions. Therefore, the OTCI Index was **not** selected; instead, an S&P 500 Index (SP) fund was selected for each of the three transactions.

Table 37B indicates the gross transaction returns during 1984 for the GFSS1 and GFSS2-selected funds. The GFSS1-selected fund was 20th Century Select fund for each transaction fund yielding a net annual return of 0%.

The GFSS2-selected fund was the S&P 500 Index fund for each transaction yielding a net annual return of 13%.

Table 38A illustrates market index selection for 1992 when both the S&P 500 and DJIA indices were considered. The DJIA index was not considered in prior years because no DJIA-based index fund was available.

The DJIA Index was selected for five of the nine transactions during the year. The OTCI Index was selected for three transactions and the S&P 500 Index was selected for one transaction.

Table 38B shows the gross transaction returns plus the net annual returns for the GFSS1 and GFSS2-selected growth funds during 1992. The GFSS1-selected fund was 20th Century Ultra for each transaction yielding a net annual return of -0.7%.

Five of these transactions were profitable. The GFSS2-selected fund varied among the S&P 500 Index, the DJIA Index and 20th Century Ultra fund. All nine transactions were profitable yielding a net annual return of 21.9%.

TABLE 37
COMPUTATION OF 1984 NET ANNUAL RETURN FOR GFSS2-SELECTED GROWTH FUNDS WHEN TIMED BY MTM6 MKTIME MODEL

A. INDEX SELECTION INDICATORS FOR EACH BUY/SELL TRANSACTION

INDEX SELECTION INDICATOR (SEE TABLE 33A)	BUY/SELL TRANSACTIONS #83-5B FM 1/01 TO 5/30	#84-1 FM 5/30 TO 7/18	#84-2 FM 7/18 TO 12/31
SP DIFF	-0.42	-1.63	-1.63
DJ DIFF	-0.91	-2.39	-1.90
SP DIFF MOVING AVERAGE	-0.41	-1.37	-0.68
DJ DIFF MOVING AVERAGE	-0.67	-1.42	-0.62
SELECTED INDEX (TABLE 33B)	SP	SP	SP

B. BUY/SELL TRANSACTION RETURNS FOR SELECTED INDEX OR GROWTH FUND

INDEX OR TOP-PERFROMING NO-LOAD GROWTH FUND FOR 1984 INVESTMENT	GROSS TRANSACTION RETURNS #83-5B FM 1/01 TO 5/30	#84-1 FM 5/30 TO 7/18	#84-2 FM 7/18 TO 12/31	NET ANNUAL RETURN ADJUSTED FOR TRADING FEES
S&P 500 INDEX	-1.1	2.0	12.7	
GFSS1-SELECTED TOP FUND*	-11.7	3.1	10.5	0.0
GFSS-2 SELECTED TOP FUND	-1.1	2.0	12.7	13.0

* 20TH CENTURY SELECT DURING 1984

TABLE 38
COMPUTATION OF 1992 NET ANNUAL RETURN FOR GFSS-2 SELECTED GROWTH FUNDS WHEN TIMED BY MTM6 MKTIME MODEL

A. INDEX SELECTION INDICATORS FOR EACH BUY/SELL TRANSACTION

INDEX SELECTION INDICATOR (SEE TABLE 33A)	BUY/SELL TRANSACTIONS #1 FM 1/01 TO 2/27	#2 FM 2/27 TO 3/18	#3 FM 3/18 TO 4/13	#4 FM 4/13 TO 5/01	#5 FM 5/01 TO 6/30	#6 FM 6/30 TO 8/28	#7 FM 8/28 TO 11/23	#8 FM 11/23 TO 12/22	#9 FM 12/22 TO 12/31
SP DIFF	0.0	-1.35	-0.53	-3.09	-1.99	-2.03	0.80	0.67	-1.03
DJ DIFF	0.13	-1.53	-0.36	-3.09	-1.80	-1.80	1.17	2.22	0.05
SP DIFF MOVING AVERAGE	-0.42	-1.75	-0.64	-3.03	-3.92	-1.86	0.45	1.43	-1.49
DJ DIFF MOVING AVERAGE	-0.24	-2.59	-0.74	-3.42	-3.94	-1.43	0.76	2.89	-0.42
SP DIFF-SP DIFF MVG AVG	0.42	0.40	0.11	-0.06	1.93	-0.17	0.35	-0.76	0.46
DJ DIFF-DJ DIFF MVG AVG	0.37	1.06	0.38	0.33	2.14	-0.37	0.42	-0.67	0.48
SELECTED INDEX (TABLE 33B)	OTCI	DJ	DJ	DJ	DJ	SP	OTCI	OTCI	DJ

B. BUY/SELL TRANSACTION RETURNS FOR SELECTED INDEX OR GROWTH FUND

INDEX OR TOP-PERFORMING NO-LOAD GROWTH FUND FOR 1992 INVESTMENT	BUY/SELL GROSS TRANSACTION RETURNS #1 FM 1/01 TO 2/27	#2 FM 2/27 TO 3/18	#3 FM 3/18 TO 4/13	#4 FM 4/13 TO 5/01	#5 FM 5/01 TO 6/30	#6 FM 6/30 TO 8/28	#7 FM 8/28 TO 11/23	#8 FM 11/23 TO 12/22	#9 FM 12/22 TO 12/31	NET ANNUAL RETURN ADJUSTED FOR TRADING FEES
S&P 500 INDEX	-0.7	-0.9	-0.6	0.9	0.6	3.4	1.6	1.9	-0.9	
DOW JONES IND. AVG	2.7	0.1	1.2	1.2	1.7	1.6	0.2	2.2	0.1	
GFSS1 TOP FUND*	1.6	-2.3	-6.8	-10.3	-0.6	4.7	9.7	3.2	3.8	-0.7
GFSS2-SELECTED TOP FUND	1.6	0.1	1.2	1.2	1.7	3.4	9.7	3.2	0.1	21.9

* 20TH CENTURY ULTRA DURING 1992

Selecting One or More of the Top Five Growth Funds

In the previous paragraphs of this section, we have described the three steps of the GFSS2 growth fund selection procedure. Upon completion of Step 3, we would have selected one of three market indices for investment when a Buy signal is generated by the mktime model. If the OTCI Index is selected, then we would invest in one or more of the top five growth funds selected annually as described in Step 2 of the selection procedure. In Tables 36, 37, and 38, we have assumed that the top (#1) growth fund was selected. We now examine the comparative performance of the top five growth funds *when timed by the MTM6 mktime model* in order to obtain guidance as to which of these five top funds to select.

Table 39 lists the 5-year MARs (mean annualized returns) of the five top growth funds when MTM6-timed during the 11-year period from 1982 through 1992. These returns have been adjusted for mutual fund trading fees. Figure 10 provides a graphic illustration of the data shown in Table 39. Table 39 and Figure 10 indicate that:

- THE #1 FUND HAD THE HIGHEST 5-YEAR MAR VALUE in the last five 5-year periods from period #3 (84-88) to period #7 (88-92).
- THE #2 FUND HAD THE SECOND HIGHEST 5-YEAR MAR value in the last four 5-year periods from period #4 (85-89) to period #7 (88-92).
- THE #4 FUND HAD THE THIRD HIGHEST 5-YEAR MAR VALUE in six out of the seven 5-year periods.

The above data suggests the following procedure for selecting one or more of the Step 2 top five growth funds when the OTCI Index has been selected under step 3:

Select the #1 growth fund for investment if no restrictions are imposed by the mutual fund as to the maximum amount that can be redeemed within a specified period.
If the #1 fund imposes restrictions as to the maximum amount that can be invested, then invest the balance of the investment account in the #2 fund.
If both the #1 and #2 funds impose restrictions, then invest the balance (if any) of the investment account in the #4 fund.

TABLE 39
5-YR MEAN ANNUALIZED RETURNS ADJUSTED FOR TRADING FEES TOP FIVE GROWTH FUNDS SELECTED BY THE GFSS2 SYSTEM (1) AND TIMED BY THE MTM6 MKTIME MODEL 11-YEAR PERIOD FROM 1982 THROUGH 1992

		TOP MTM6-TIMED GROWTH FUNDS [NOTE 1]				
YEAR	S&P 500 INDEX BUY/HOLD RETURN	#1	#2	#3	#4	#5
82-86	19.9	33.2	25.5	30.9	34.3	29.1
83-87	16.5	30.9	26.6	30.7	31.8	26.8
84-88	15.3	33.7	29.4	31.1	31.0	29.7
85-89	20.4	41.6	37.0	33.3	35.5	34.5
86-90	13.2	41.2	38.2	30.0	33.5	31.0
87-91	15.3	47.1	42.4	31.7	35.8	31.6
88-92	15.9	43.2	38.7	28.9	33.2	29.3

NOTES:

1. SEE TABLE 32 FOR A BRIEF DESCRIPTION OF THE GFSS2 GROWTH FUND SELECTION SYSTEM. THE TOP FIVE GROWTH FUNDS ARE SELECTED AS DESCRIBED UNDER STEP 2.

FIGURE 10

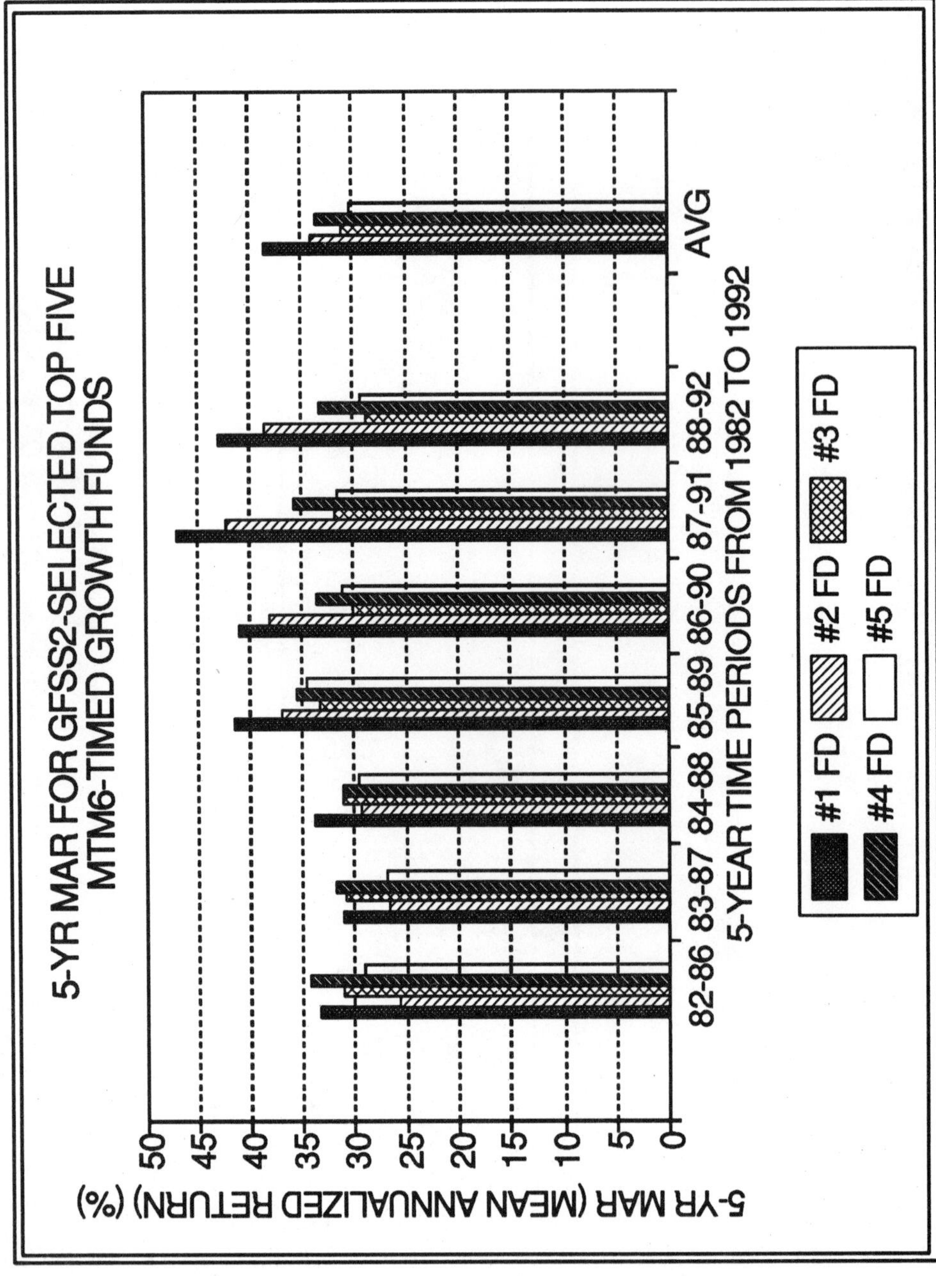
5-YR MAR FOR GFSS2-SELECTED TOP FIVE
MTM6-TIMED GROWTH FUNDS
5-YR MAR (MEAN ANNUALIZED RETURN) (%)
50
45
40
35
30
25
20
15
10
5
0
82-86
83-87
84-88
85-89
86-90
87-91
88-92
AVG
5-YEAR TIME PERIODS FROM 1982 TO 1992
#1 FD
#2 FD
#3 FD
#4 FD
#5 FD

6: PERFORMANCE EVALUATION OF THE TOP-PERFORMING INVESTMENT SYSTEMS

Introduction

In Chapter 4, we described how the five 1992 top-performing mktime models were selected for investment during 1992. We also made a preliminary selection of the five AMFI mktime models as the five 1993 top-performing mktime models. In Chapter 5, we described the GFSS2 growth fund selection system for use with mktime models MTM4/5/6. For use with mktime models MTM2 and 3, we selected the S&P 500 Index until a superior growth fund selection system becomes available. In this section, we present the hypothetical performance of the five 1993 top-performing investment systems during the 11-year period from 1982 through 1992.

The hypothetical performance of these systems is determined by computer back-testing. Each mktime model is described by precisely defined rules for generating Buy and Sell signals. Each growth fund selection system is also described by precisely defined rules for selecting the best growth fund when a Buy signal is generated. These rules are used to determine what decisions would have been made in the past based upon market conditions at that time. The adjective "hypothetical" is used to indicate that no actual investments were made using these investment systems.

System Nomenclature

In Chapters 4 and 5, we have assigned shorthand nomenclature to the top-performing mktime models (MTM1 to MTM6) and to the latest growth fund selection system (GFSS2), respectively. Table 40 indicates the shorthand nomenclature for mutual fund investment systems based upon their mktime model and their growth fund or growth fund selection system. Using the nomenclature defined in Table 40, the SYS62 system is applicable to the system wherein a GFSS2-selected growth fund is timed by the MTM6 mktime model. The SYS201 system employs the S&P 500 Index timed by the MTM2 mktime model.

TABLE 40
MUTUAL FUND INVESTMENT SYSTEM NOMENCLATURE

A. BASIC NOMENCLATURE

SYSTEM ID	MKTIME MODEL	GTH FD OR GFSS (1)
SYSxy	x	y

B. x VALUES

x	MKTIME MODEL
1	MTM1
2	MTM2
3	MTM3
4	MTM4
5	MTM5
6	MTM6

C. y VALUES

y	GTH FUND OR GFSS (NOTE 1)
01	S&P 500 INDEX
02	DJIA INDEX (2)
03	OTCI INDEX (3)
1	GFSS1
2	GFSS2

NOTES:

1. GFSS = GROWTH FUND SELECTION SYSTEM
2. DJIA = DOW JONES INDUSTRIAL AVERAGE
3. OTCI = OVER-THE-COUNTER INDUSTRIAL (NASDAQ)

The Five 1993 Top-Performing Investment Systems

Table 41 indicates the five 1993 top-performing mutual fund investment systems for which 11-year hypothetical performance data will be presented in the following paragraphs. The first four systems (SYS62, 52, 301, and 201) were also the four 1992 top-performing systems. The fifth 1992 top-performing system was provided by the *Investors Intelligence* newsletter. At this time (January 1993), the 1992 performance data for mktime newsletters and for audited market timers is not available. Consequently, we are including SYS42 (GFSS2-selected fund timed by the MTM4 mktime model) in the top-five-system list on a tentative basis.

System Evaluation Criteria

Chapter 2 described a set of investment system performance criteria for evaluating the investment systems described herein. Two types of criteria are described; namely, "return" and "risk" criteria. Both types are used to select the preferred system for investment. The "risk" criteria are also used to monitor the selected system's performance so as to determine if and when the selected system is not performing as expected based upon past performance. In the following paragraphs, each of the systems listed in Table 41 will be described in terms of these evaluation criteria.

System 62 Performance Evaluation

As indicated in Table 41, System 62 uses a GFSS2-selected growth fund in conjunction with the MTM6 mktime model. Its hypothetical performance data is presented in Figure 11 and Tables 42,43 and 44 for the 11-year period from 1982 through 1992.

- Figure 11 and Table 42 indicate the annual and mean annualized returns of the system and of the S&P 500 Index when bought and held.
- Table 43 lists the returns (adjusted for trading fees) of the 61 Buy/Sell transactions during the 11-year period.
- Table 44 summarizes the overall performance of the system in terms of the "return" and "risk" performance criteria described in Chapter 2.

TABLE 41
THE 1993 TOP-PERFORMING INVESTMENT SYSTEMS (1)

MUTUAL FUND INVESTMENT SYSTEM	MKTIME MODEL (NOTE 2)	GROWTH FUND OR GFSS (NOTE 3)
SYS62	MTM6	GFSS2
SYS52	MTM5	GFSS2
SYS301	MTM3	S&P 500 INDEX
SYS201	MTM2	S&P 500 INDEX
SYS42	MTM4	GFSS2
SYS101	MTM1 (BUY/HOLD)	S&P 500 INDEX

NOTES:

- 1. THIS LISTING IS PRELIMINARY AT THIS TIME (JANUARY 1993) AND IS SUBJECT TO CHANGE AFTER 1993 EVALUATION OF MKTIME NEWSLETTERS AND AUDITED MARKET TIMERS.
- 2. SEE TABLE 22 FOR DESCRIPTION OF MKTIME MODELS.
- 3. SEE TABLE 32 FOR DESCRIPTION OF GFSS2 GROWTH FUND SELECTION SYSTEM.

FIGURE 11
ANNUAL RETURNS (82-92) & 11/5-YR MAR 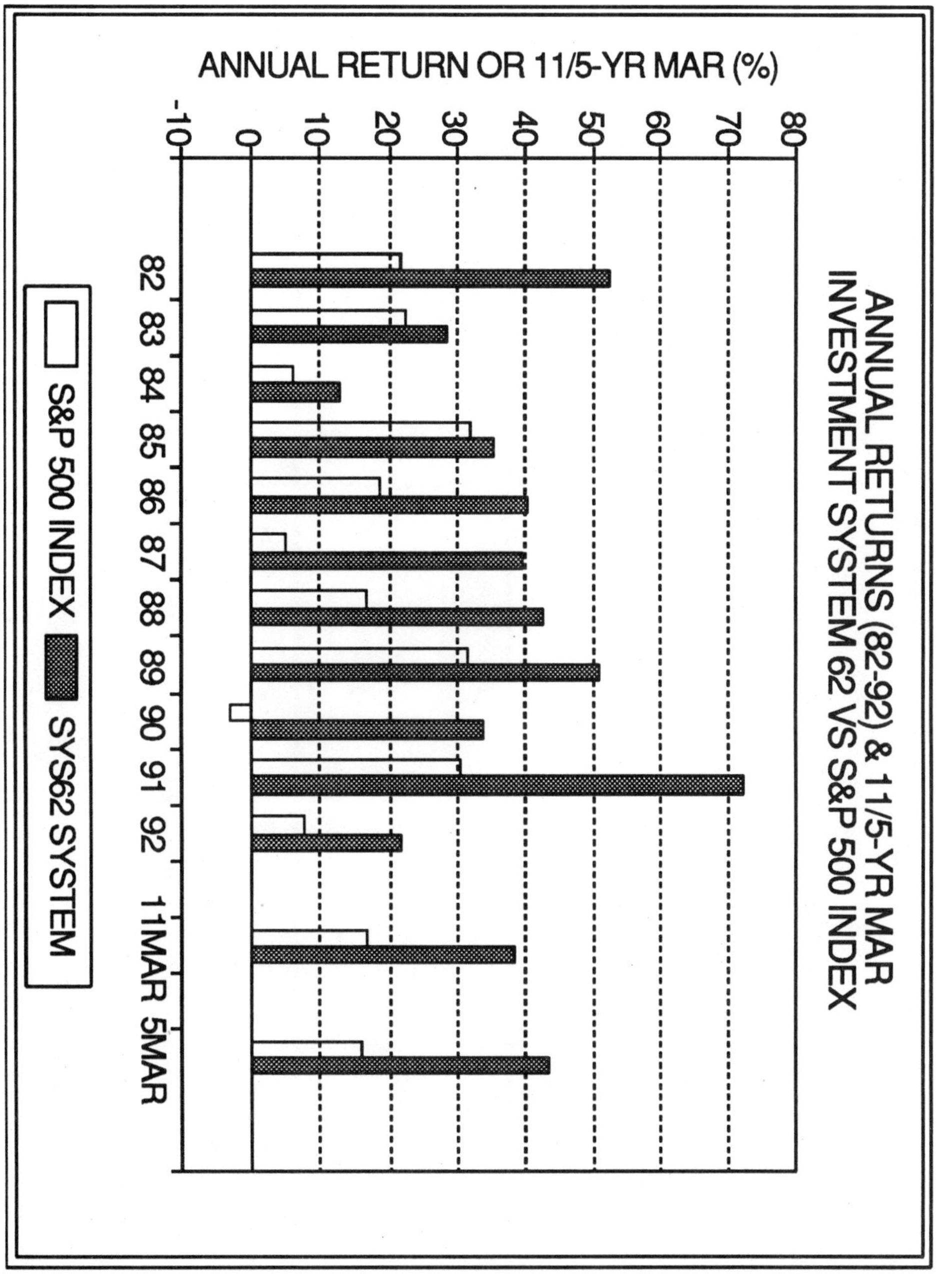
INVESTMENT SYSTEM 62 VS S&P 500 INDEX
ANNUAL RETURN OR 11/5-YR MAR (%)
-10
0
10
20
30
40
50
60
70
80
82 83 84 85 86 87 88 89 90 91 92 11MAR 5MAR
S&P 500 INDEX
SYS62 SYSTEM

TABLE 42
ANNUAL RETURNS ADJUSTED FOR TRADING FEES (%)
SYSTEM 62 (GFSS2-SELECTED TOP FUND WHEN MTM6-TIMED) VS S&P 500 INDEX
11-YEAR PERIOD FROM 1982 THROUGH 1992

YEAR	S&P 500 INDEX BUY/HOLD RETURN	SYS62 TOP-FD RETURN
1982	21.6	52.5
1983	22.5	28.3
1984	6.2	13.0
1985	31.8	35.4
1986	18.8	40.2
1987	5.2	39.5
1988	16.6	42.6
1989	31.7	50.7
1990	-3.1	33.7
1991	30.5	72.0
1992	7.7	21.9
11MAR (82-92)	16.7	38.3
5MAR (88-92)	15.9	43.2

TABLE 43
BUY/SELL TRANSACTION RETURNS ADJUSTED FOR TRADING FEES
SYSTEM 62 (GFSS2-SELECTED TOP FUND WHEN MTM6-TIMED)
11-YEAR PERIOD FROM 1982 THROUGH 1992

NOTE: A BUY/SELL TRANSACTION BEGINS WHEN A BUY SIGNAL IS EXECUTED AND ENDS WHEN THE NEXT BUY SIGNAL IS EXECUTED. IT INCLUDES A BUY PERIOD (GROWTH FUND INVESTMENT) AND A SELL PERIOD (MONEY MARKET FUND INVESTMENT).

	BUY/SELL TRANSACTION NUMBER								
YEAR	#1	#2	#3	#4	#5	#6	#7	#8	# PROFITABLE XSNS
1982	-3.3	-2.5	14.5	42.9					2
1983	-0.2	4.7	17.2	2.4	-0.1				3
1984	1.7	23.8							2
1985	-0.4	4.0	0.8	0.2	-0.1	19.9			4
1986	19.2	-1.5	7.4	1.6	4.5	0.3	4.1	22.3	7
1987	-0.1	7.7	-0.1	0.5	3.1	7.5			4
1988	18.8	6.0	3.4	-0.6	2.9	11.0			5
1989	17.9	1.5	4.8	-0.3	4.0	3.0	1.8		6
1990	6.8	4.6	1.8	18.6	0.2				5
1991	37.0	0.8	-0.8	6.0	19.8				4
1992	-0.1	2.2	1.4	3.2	9.8	3.0	-0.1		5
TOTAL NUMBER OF PROFITABLE TRANSACTIONS									47
TOTAL NUMBER OF ALL TRANSACTIONS									61
PERCENTAGE OF PROFITABLE TRANSACTIONS									77

TABLE 44
HYPOTHETICAL PERFORMANCE SUMMARY
SYSTEM 62 (GFSS2-SELECTED TOP FUND WHEN MTM6-TIMED)
11-YEAR PERIOD FROM 1982 THROUGH 1992

A. "RETURN" PERFORMANCE CRITERIA (%)		
	INVESTMENT SYSTEM CONSISTING OF: GTH FD OR GFSS (1) / MKTIME MODEL (2)	
PERFORMANCE CRITERION	SYS101 S&P 500/ MTM1	SYS 62 GFSS2/MTM6
MEAN ANNUALIZED RETURN (MAR)	16.7	38.3
AVERAGE % OF PROFITABLE BUY/SELL TRANSACTIONS (APT)	NA	77.0
MEAN TRANSACTION RETURN (MTR)	NA	6.1
B. "RISK" PERFORMANCE CRITERIA		
MINIMUM ANNUAL RETURN OR MAXIMUM ANNUAL LOSS (82-91)	-3.1	13.0
MINIMUM % OF PROFITABLE BUY/SELL TRANSACTIONS (MPT) (NOTE 3)	NA	62.5
MINIMUM TRANACTION RETURN OR MAXIMUM TRANACTION LOSS (MTL)	NA	-3.3

NOTES:

1. GFSS = GROWTH FUND SELECTION SYSTEM; SEE TABLE 32 FOR A BRIEF DESCRIPTION OF THE GFSS2 GROWTH FUND SELECTION SYSTEM.
2. SEE TABLE 22 FOR A BRIEF DESCRIPTION OF THE TOP-PERFORMING MKTIME MODELS. THE MTM1 MODEL IS BUY & HOLD.
3. DURING THE LAST EIGHT (8) TRANSACTIONS.

"Return" Performance Evaluation

Figure 11 and Tables 42, 43 and 44 show that:

- System 62 had higher annual returns than the S&P 500 Index by a significant margin in EVERY YEAR DURING THE 11-YEAR PERIOD.
- SYSTEM 62 HAD SUBSTANTIALLY HIGHER TOTAL 11-YEAR RETURNS THAN THE INDEX as indicated by the following comparisons:

MAR	38% vs. 17%
Inflation-Adjusted Total Return	2000% vs. 220%
End-of-period inflation-adjusted market value of $1,000 lump sum investment	$21,000 vs $ 3,200

- 47 (77%) of the Buy/Sell Transaction were profitable.

"Risk" Performance Evaluation

Tables 43 and 44 show that:

- System 62 maximum transaction loss during the 11-year period was 3.3% (1982 transaction #1).
- System 62 minimum percentage of profitable transactions (during the previous eight transactions) was 63%.

These "risk" performance values can be used to monitor System 62 performance on an ongoing basis, as follows:

- If the loss during the Buy cycle of a transaction exceeds the maximum transaction loss (3.3%), then an investor should switch his assets to a money market fund the next day; i.e. without waiting for a Sell signal.
- If the percentage of profitable transactions during the last eight transactions drops below the minimum percentage (63%), then an investor should switch assets to a money market fund. Assets should remain in the money market fund until the problem is diagnosed and corrected or switched to another investment system.

System 52 Performance Evaluation

As indicated in Table 41, System 52 uses a GFSS2-selected growth fund in conjunction with the MTM5 mktime model. Its hypothetical performance data is presented in Figure 12 and Tables 45, 46 and 47 for the 11-year period from 1982 through 1992.

- Figure 12 and Table 45 indicate the annual and mean annualized returns of the system and of the S&P 500 Index when bought and held.
- Table 46 lists the returns (adjusted for trading fees) of the 50 Buy/Sell transactions generated by the system during the 11-year period.
- Table 47 summarizes the overall performance of the system in terms of the "return" and "risk" performance criteria described in Chapter 2.

"Return" Performance Evaluation

Figure 12 and Tables 45, 46 and 47 show that:

- System 52 had higher annual returns than the S&P 500 Index by a significant margin in EVERY YEAR EXCEPT 1983.
- SYSTEM 52 HAD SUBSTANTIALLY HIGHER TOTAL 11-YEAR RETURNS than the index as indicated by the following comparisons:

MAR	32% vs. 17%
Inflation-adjusted total return	1100% vs. 220%
End-of-period inflation-adjusted market value of $1,000 lump sum investment	$12,000 vs. $ 3,200

- 40 (80%) of the Buy/Sell transactions were profitable.

"Risk" Performance Evaluation

Tables 46 and 47 show that:

- System 52 maximum transaction loss during the 11-year period was 2.8% (1982 transaction #1).
- System 52 minimum percentage of profitable transactions (during the previous eight transactions) was 63%.

FIGURE 12

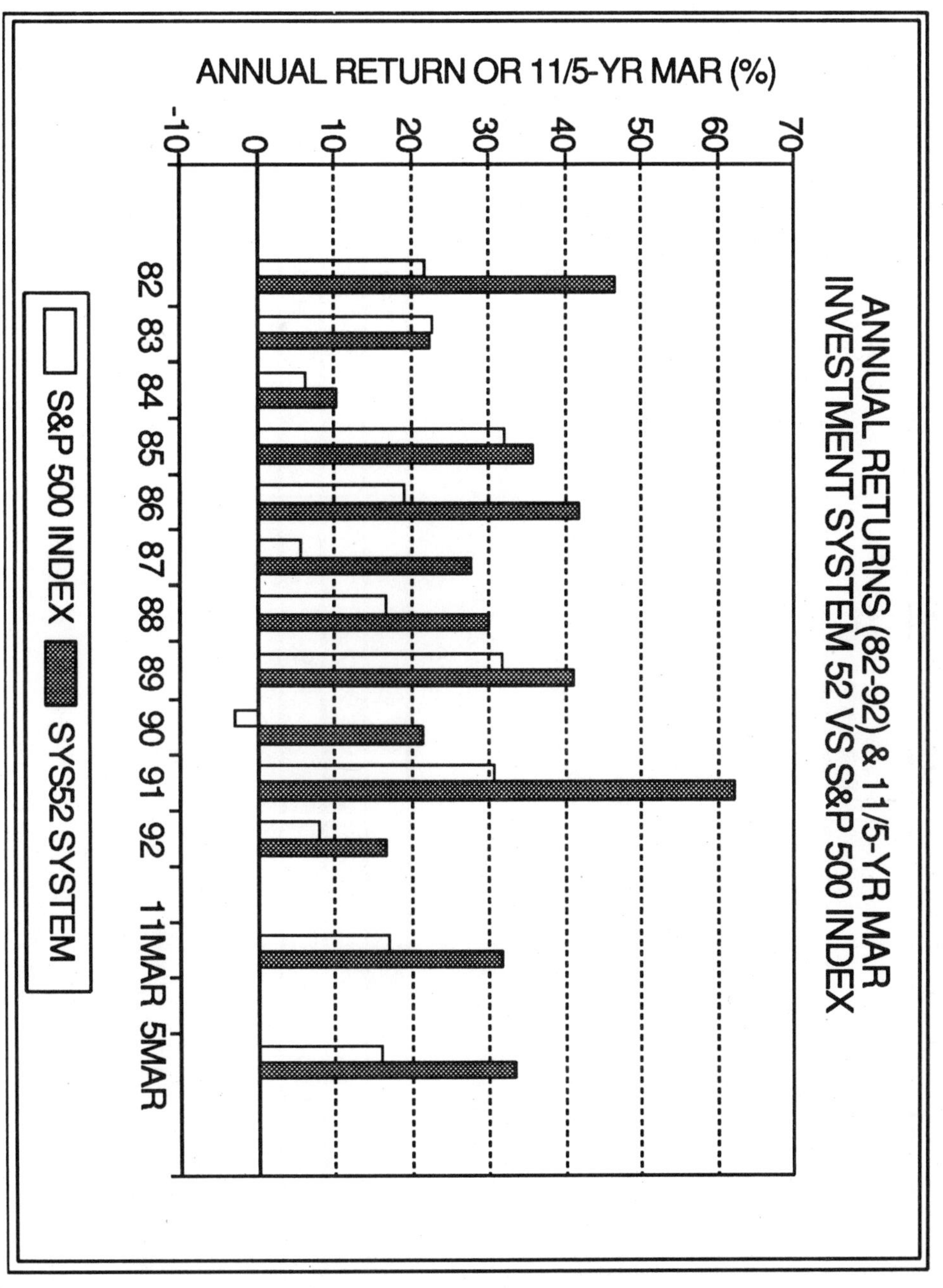
ANNUAL RETURNS (82-92) & 11/5-YR MAR
INVESTMENT SYSTEM 52 VS S&P 500 INDEX
ANNUAL RETURN OR 11/5-YR MAR (%)
-10
0
10
20
30
40
50
60
70
82
83
84
85
86
87
88
89
90
91
92
11MAR
5MAR
S&P 500 INDEX
SYS52 SYSTEM

TABLE 45
ANNUAL RETURNS ADJUSTED FOR TRADING FEES (%)
SYSTEM 52 (GFSS2-SELECTED TOP FUND WHEN MTM5-TIMED) VS S&P 500 INDEX
11-YEAR PERIOD FROM 1982 THROUGH 1992

YEAR	S&P 500 INDEX BUY/HOLD RETURN	SYS52 TOP-FD RETURN
1982	21.6	46.3
1983	22.5	22.2
1984	6.2	10.3
1985	31.8	35.7
1986	18.8	41.9
1987	5.2	27.7
1988	16.6	30.1
1989	31.7	40.9
1990	-3.1	21.1
1991	30.5	61.8
1992	7.7	16.6
11MAR (82-92)	16.7	31.5
5MAR (88-92)	15.9	33.2

TABLE 46
BUY/SELL TRANSACTION RETURNS ADJUSTED FOR TRADING FEES (%) FOR SYSTEM 52 (GFSS2-SELECTED TOP FUND WHEN MTM5-TIMED): 11-YEAR PERIOD FROM 1982 THROUGH 1992

NOTE: A BUY/SELL TRANSACTION BEGINS WHEN A BUY SIGNAL IS EXECUTED AND ENDS WHEN THE NEXT BUY SIGNAL IS EXECUTED. IT INCLUDES A BUY PERIOD (GROWTH FUND INVESTMENT) AND A SELL PERIOD (MONEY MARKET FUND INVESTMENT).

	BUY/SELL TRANSACTION NUMBER								
YEAR	#1	#2	#3	#4	#5	#6	#7	#8	# PROFITABLE XSNS
1982	-2.8	-1.3	17.5	28.0					2
1983	2.4	17.3	2.4	0.0					3
1984	-0.8	24.1							1
1985	5.3	-0.1	19.9						2
1986	19.5	7.8	4.5	0.3	4.1				5
1987	-0.2	16.8	-0.1	7.1	2.0	0.1	0.3		5
1988	0.2	18.8	6.1	0.5	3.0				5
1989	-0.1	8.1	18.2	5.6	2.0	1.1	1.2		6
1990	-0.2	5.4	16.5						2
1991	0.2	37.5	-0.8	6.1	13.6				4
1992	1.0	1.0	1.4	3.4	7.5				5
TOTAL NUMBER OF PROFITABLE TRANSACTIONS									40
TOTAL NUMBER OF ALL TRANSACTIONS									50
PERCENTAGE OF PROFITABLE TRANSACTIONS									80

TABLE 47
HYPOTHETICAL PERFORMANCE SUMMARY
SYSTEM 52 (GFSS2-SELECTED TOP FUND WHEN MTM5-TIMED)
11-YEAR PERIOD FROM 1982 THROUGH 1992

A. "RETURN" PERFORMANCE CRITERIA (%)		
	INVESTMENT SYSTEM CONSISTING OF: GTH FD OR GFSS (1) / MKTIME MODEL	
PERFORMANCE CRITERION	SYS101 S&P 500/ MTM1	SYS52 GFSS2/MTM5
MEAN ANNUALIZED RETURN (MAR)	16.7	31.5
AVERAGE % OF PROFITABLE BUY/SELL TRANSACTIONS (APT)	NA	80.0
MEAN TRANSACTION RETURN (MTR)	NA	6.1
B. "RISK" PERFORMANCE CRITERIA		
MINIMUM ANNUAL RETURN OR MAXIMUM ANNUAL LOSS (82-92)	-3.1	10.3
MINIMUM % OF PROFITABLE BUY/SELL TRANSACTIONS (MPT) (NOTE 3)	NA	62.5
MININUM TRANSACTION RETURN OR MAXIMUM TRANSACTION LOSS (MTL)	NA	-2.8

NOTES:

1. GFSS = GROWTH FUND SELECTION SYSTEM; SEE TABLE 32 FOR A BRIEF DESCRIPTION OF THE GFSS2 GROWTH FUND SELECTION SYSTEM.
2. SEE TABLE 22 FOR A BRIEF DESCRIPTION OF THE TOP-PERFORMING MKTIME MODELS. THE MTM1 MODEL IS BUY & HOLD.
3. DURING THE LAST EIGHT (8) TRANSACTIONS

These "risk" performance values can be used to monitor System 52 performance on an ongoing basis in the same manner as described in Chapter 6 for System 62.

System 301 Performance Evaluation

As indicated in Table 41, System 301 is based upon the S&P 500 Index timed by mktime model MTM3. Its hypothetical performance data is shown in Figure 13 and Table 48 for the 11-year period from 1982 through 1992. No data is presented for the Buy/Sell transaction returns because the number of transactions per year is small.

- Figure 13 and Table 48 present the annual and mean annualized returns of the system and of the S&P 500 Index when bought and held. The figure and table show that:
- System 301 had higher annual returns than the index during three years, namely, 1982, 1984 and 1987.
- System 301 had higher total 11-year returns than the index as indicated by the following comparisons:

MAR	19% vs. 17%
Inflation-adjusted total return	300% vs. 220%
End-of-period inflation-adjusted market value of $1,000 lump sum investment	$4,000 vs. $3,200

- System 301 had a higher minimum annual return (-0.5%) than the index (-3.1%).

System 201 Performance Evaluation

As indicated in Table 41, System 201 is based upon the S&P 500 Index timed by mktime model MTM2. Its hypothetical performance data is shown in Figure 13 and Table 48 for the 11-year period from 1982 through 1992. No data is presented for the Buy/Sell transaction returns because there were only two transactions during the 11-year period.

- Figure 14 and Table 49 present the annual and mean annualized returns of the system and of the S&P 500 Index when bought and held. The figure and table show that:
- System 201 had the same annual returns as the index during every year except 1987 and 1992. The system had a

FIGURE 13

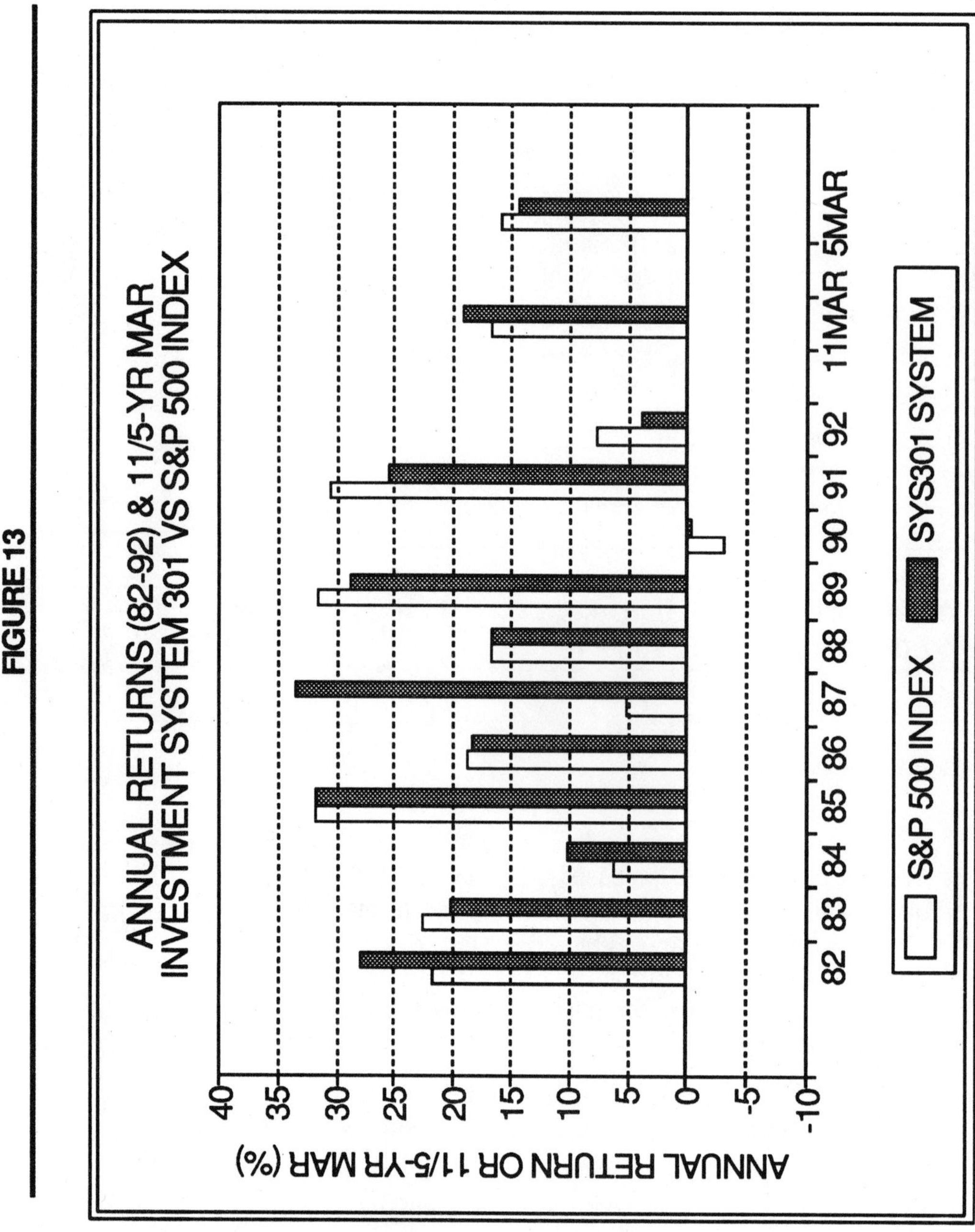

ANNUAL RETURNS (82-92) & 11/5-YR MAR
INVESTMENT SYSTEM 301 VS S&P 500 INDEX
ANNUAL RETURN OR 11/5-YR MAR (%)
40
35
30
25
20
15
10
5
0
-5
-10
82 83 84 85 86 87 88 89 90 91 92 11MAR 5MAR
S&P 500 INDEX
SYS301 SYSTEM

TABLE 48
ANNUAL RETURNS ADJUSTED FOR TRADING FEES (%)
SYSTEM 301 (S&P 500 INDEX WHEN MTM3-TIMED) VS INDEX WHEN BOUGHT/HELD
11-YEAR PERIOD FROM 1982 THROUGH 1992

YEAR	S&P 500 INDEX BUY/HOLD RETURN	SYS301 TOP-FD RETURN
1982	21.6	28.1
1983	22.5	20.2
1984	6.2	10.2
1985	31.8	31.8
1986	18.8	18.4
1987	5.2	33.4
1988	16.6	16.6
1989	31.7	28.8
1990	-3.1	-0.5
1991	30.5	25.4
1992	7.7	3.8
11MAR (82-92)	16.7	19.2
5MAR (88-92)	15.9	14.2

FIGURE 14

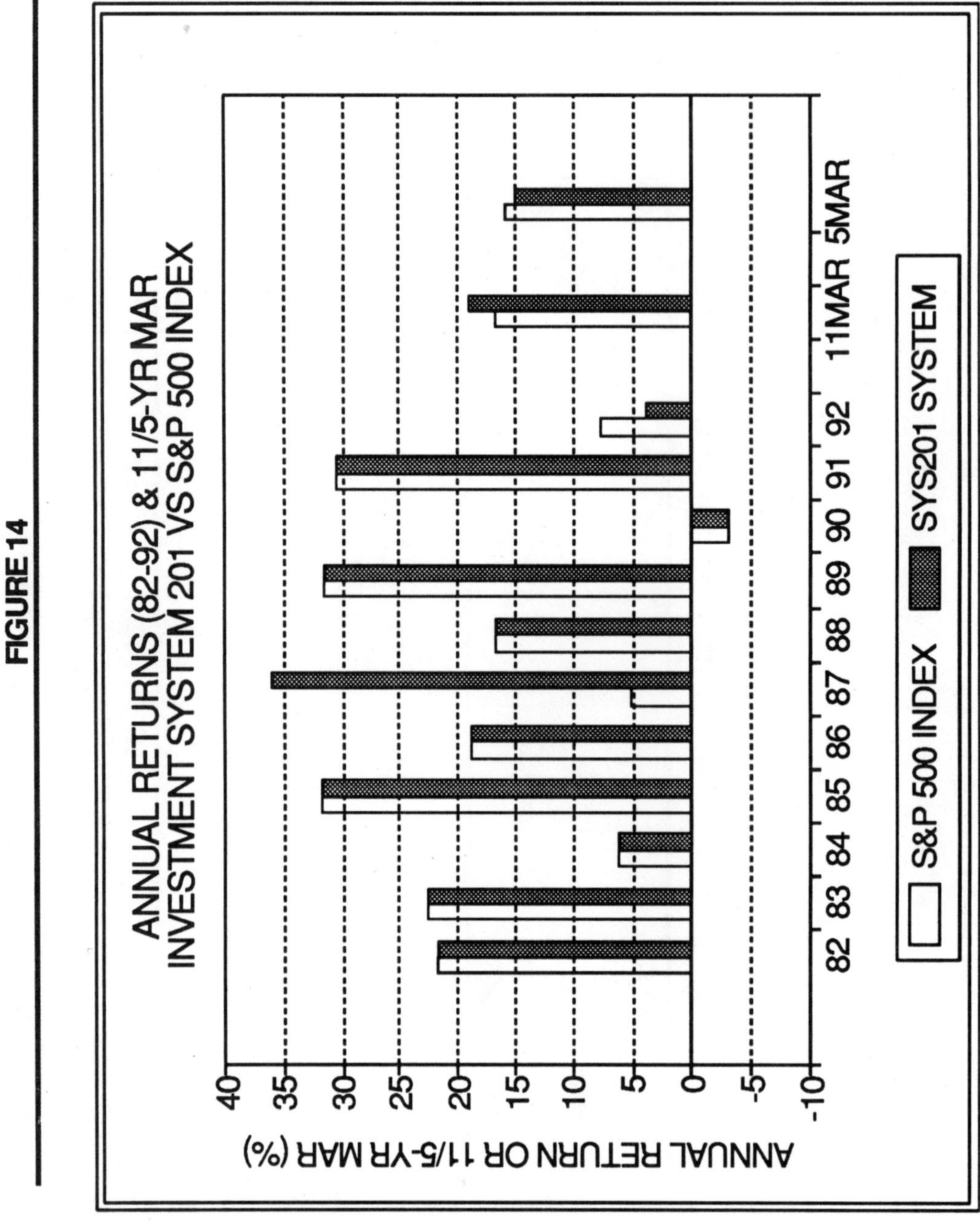
ANNUAL RETURNS (82-92) & 11/5-YR MAR
INVESTMENT SYSTEM 201 VS S&P 500 INDEX
ANNUAL RETURN OR 11/5-YR MAR (%)
40
35
30
25
20
15
10
5
0
-5
-10
82 83 84 85 86 87 88 89 90 91 92 11MAR 5MAR
S&P 500 INDEX
SYS201 SYSTEM

TABLE 49
ANNUAL RETURNS ADJUSTED FOR TRADING FEES (%)
SYSTEM 201 (S&P 500 INDEX WHEN MTM2-TIMED) VS INDEX WHEN BOUGHT/HELD
11-YEAR PERIOD FROM 1982 THROUGH 1992

YEAR	S&P 500 INDEX BUY/HOLD RETURN	SYS201 TOP-FD RETURN
1982	21.6	21.6
1983	22.5	22.5
1984	6.2	6.2
1985	31.8	31.8
1986	18.8	18.8
1987	5.2	36.0
1988	16.6	16.6
1989	31.7	31.7
1990	-3.1	-3.1
1991	30.5	30.5
1992	7.7	3.8
11MAR (82-92)	16.7	19.0
5MAR (88-92)	15.9	15.1

significantly higher return in 1987; in 1992, the system had a lower annual return.

- System 201 had higher total 11-year returns than the index as indicated by the following comparisons:

MAR	19% vs. 17%
Inflation-adjusted total return	300% vs. 220%
End-of-period inflation-adjusted market value of $1,000 lump sum investment	$4,000 vs. $3,200

System 42 Performance Evaluation

As indicated in Table 41, System 42 uses a GFSS2-selected growth fund in conjunction with the MTM4 mktime model. Its hypothetical performance data is presented in Figure 15 and Table 50, 51 A and B and 52 for the 11-year period from 1982 through 1992.

Figure 15 and Table 50 present the annual and mean annualized returns of the system and of the S&P 500 Index when bought and held.

- Table 51 (A and B) list the returns (adjusted for trading fees) of the 174 Buy/Sell transactions generated by the system during the 11-year period.
- Table 52 summarizes the overall performance of the system in terms of the "return" and ":risk" criteria described in Section 2.5.

"Return" Performance Evaluation

Figure 15 and Tables 50, 51A/B and 52 show that this system's performance during the first 5-year period (82-86) and the second 5-year period (87-91) differed markedly. The mean annualized returns for the system and the S&P 500 Index during these 5-year periods and the 11-year (82-92) period were as follows:

	MEAN ANNUALIZED RETURN (%)	
Period	*S&P Index*	*System 42*
1982 - 1986	19.9	10.6
1987 - 1991	15.4	25.3
1982 - 1992	**16.7**	**17.0**

FIGURE 15

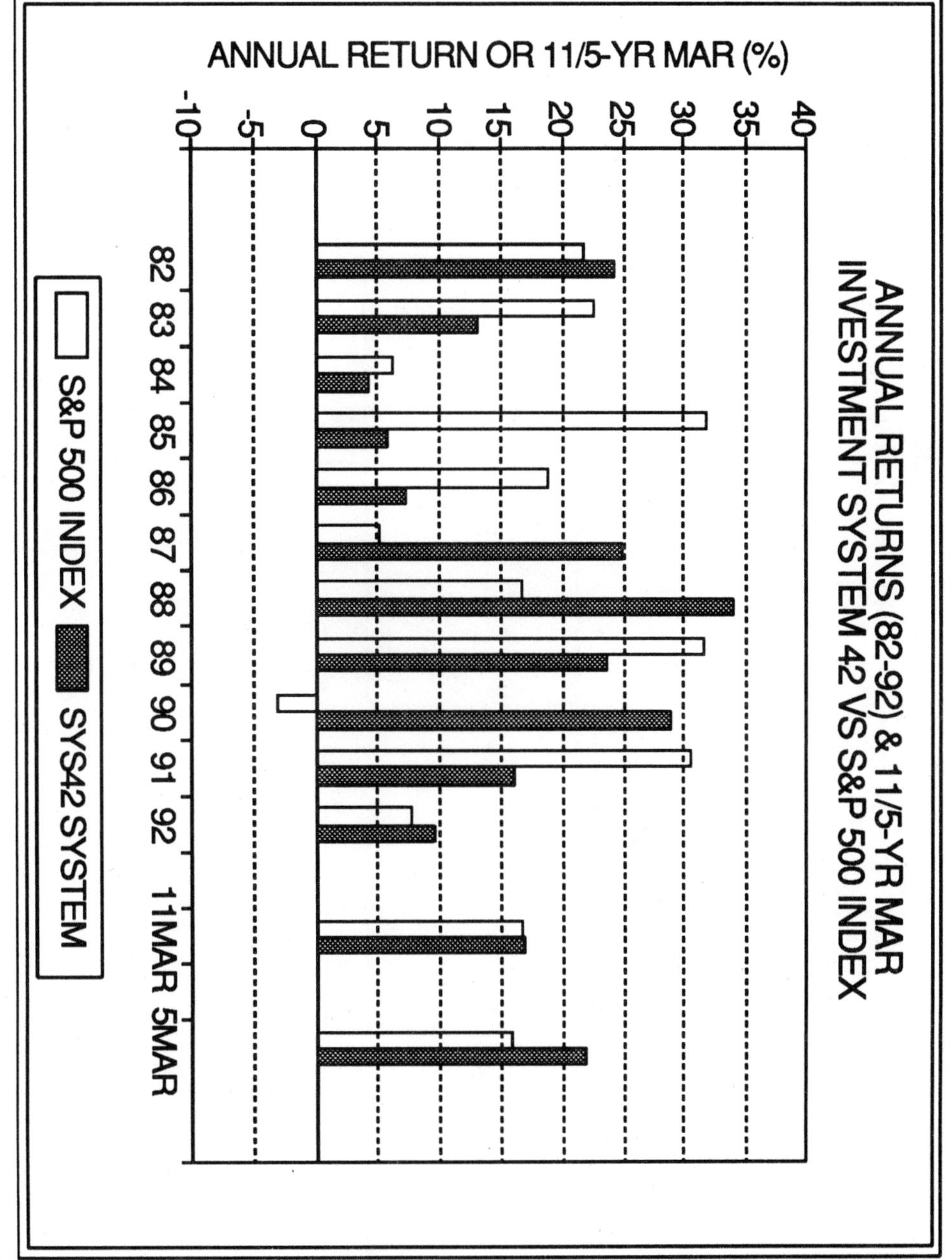
ANNUAL RETURNS (82-92) & 11/5-YR MAR
INVESTMENT SYSTEM 42 VS S&P 500 INDEX
ANNUAL RETURN OR 11/5-YR MAR (%)
-10
-5
0
5
10
15
20
25
30
35
40
82
83
84
85
86
87
88
89
90
91
92
11MAR
5MAR
S&P 500 INDEX
SYS42 SYSTEM

TABLE 50
ANNUAL RETURNS ADJUSTED FOR TRADING FEES (%)
SYSTEM 42 (GFSS2-SELECTED TOP FUND WHEN MTM4-TIMED) VS S&P 500 INDEX
11-YEAR PERIOD FROM 1982 THROUGH 1992

YEAR	S&P 500 INDEX BUY/HOLD RETURN	SYS42 TOP-FD RETURN
1982	21.6	24.2
1983	22.5	13.0
1984	6.2	4.2
1985	31.8	5.8
1986	18.8	7.1
1987	5.2	24.8
1988	16.6	33.8
1989	31.7	23.6
1990	-3.1	28.8
1991	30.5	16.0
1992	7.7	9.4
11MAR (82-92)	16.7	17.0
5MAR (88-92)	15.9	22.0

TABLE 51A
BUY/SELL TRANSACTION RETURNS ADJUSTED FOR TRADING FEES (%)
SYSTEM 42 (GFSS2-SELECTED TOP FUND WHEN MTM4-TIMED)
11-YEAR PERIOD FROM 1982 THROUGH 1992

NOTE: A BUY/SELL TRANSACTION BEGINS WHEN A BUY SIGNAL IS EXECUTED AND ENDS WHEN THE NEXT BUY SIGNAL IS EXECUTED. IT INCLUDES A BUY PERIOD (GROWTH FUND INVESTMENT) AND A SELL PERIOD (MONEY MARKET FUND INVESTMENT).

	BUY/SELL TRANSACTION NUMBER								
YEAR	**#1**	**#2**	**#3**	**#4**	**#5**	**#6**	**#7**	**#8**	**#9**
1982	-3.8	-2.0	0.5	-2.2	3.4	3.3	-2.0	-1.9	-4.1
1983	0.1	-0.5	5.0	-0.9	1.3	1.6	1.0	-1.7	3.8
1984	-2.5	-0.3	0.1	-5.7	0.1	0.0	-1.2	3.6	-0.5
1985	2.7	-1.1	0.4	0.1	0.3	-0.6	2.0	0.8	-0.2
1986	1.9	1.4	-0.5	-2.3	-1.4	3.0	-0.7	1.8	0.3
1987	2.4	1.4	0.7	6.3	3.0	2.9	0.4	1.7	0.1
1988	-0.5	1.0	3.3	4.1	0.3	4.8	1.0	2.6	1.7
1989	1.6	1.2	4.2	-0.8	-0.2	-0.3	2.0	2.0	0.9
1990	8.0	0.1	4.8	0.2	0.8	5.8	-1.5	-0.8	2.1
1991	7.3	0.0	8.1	2.4	1.0	0.2	-4.0	0.0	0.8
1992	3.6	-2.3	-0.8	-0.1	1.7	1.0	-0.4	0.0	0.1

TABLE 51B
BUY/SELL TRANSACTION RETURNS ADJUSTED FOR TRADING FEES (%)
SYSTEM 42 (GFSS2-SELECTED TOP FUND WHEN MTM4-TIMED)
11-YEAR PERIOD FROM 1982 THROUGH 1992

NOTE: A BUY/SELL TRANSACTION BEGINS WHEN A BUY SIGNAL IS EXECUTED AND ENDS WHEN THE NEXT BUY SIGNAL IS EXECUTED. IT INCLUDES A BUY PERIOD (GROWTH FUND INVESTMENT) AND A SELL PERIOD (MONEY MARKET FUND INVESTMENT).

BUY/SELL TRANSACTION NUMBERS

YEAR	#10	#11	#12	#13	#14	#15	#16	#17	# PROFITABLE XSNS
1982	5.5	5.5	10.2	0.8	10.5	0.8	3.2		10
1983	2.2	-0.3	0.1	-1.2	-0.5	2.8			9
1984	8.9	-1.2	-1.8	2.3	0.6	-0.5	0.0	-2.3	6
1985	-0.1	1.4	3.0	2.9	-2.0	2.3			10
1986	-0.9	3.0	0.6	2.4	-0.9	4.6			9
1987	1.5	-2.3	-0.7	3.0	3.0	-6.7	2.2	8.9	14
1988	0.2	-0.6	1.2	2.7	-0.2	3.1			12
1989	-0.3	4.4	0.0	0.3	1.6	1.2	3.6		11
1990	-2.6	-1.3	2.8	3.4	-2.0	5.9	-2.0	-7.8	10
1991	-3.4	-1.0	-0.7	6.6	3.8	5.2			8
1992	-1.8	3.2	-2.0	1.1	3.0	0.7	1.9		9
TOTAL NUMBER OF PROFITABLE TRANSACTIONS									108
TOTAL NUMBER OF ALL TRANSACTIONS									174
PERCENTAGE OF PROFITABLE TRANSACTIONS									62

TABLE 52
HYPOTHETICAL PERFORMANCE SUMMARY
SYSTEM 42 (GFSS2-SELECTED TOP FUND WHEN MTM4-TIMED)
11-YEAR PERIOD FROM 1982 THROUGH 1992

	INVESTMENT SYSTEM CONSISTING OF: GTH FD OR GFSS (1) /MKTIME MODEL (2)	
PERFORMANCE CRITERION	**SYS101 S&P 500/MTM1**	**SYS42 GFSS2/MTM4**
A. "RETURN" PERFORMANCE CRITERIA (%)		
MEAN ANNUALIZED RETURN (MAR)	16.7	17.0
AVERAGE % OF PROFITABLE BUY/SELL TRANSACTIONS (APT)	NA	62.0
MEAN TRANSACTION RETURN (MTR)	NA	1.0
B. "RISK" PERFORMANCE CRITERIA		
MINIMUM ANNUAL RETURN OR MAXIMUM ANNUAL LOSS (82-91)	-3.1	4.2
MINIMUM % OF PROFITABLE BUY/SELL TRANSACTIONS (MPT) (NOTE 3)	NA	25.0
MINIMUM TRANSACTION RETURN OR MAXIMUM TRANSACTION LOSS (MTL)	NA	-7.8

NOTES:

1:GFSS = GROWTH FUND SELECTION SYSTEM: SEE TABLE 32 FOR A BRIEF DESCRIPTION OF THE GFSS2 GROWTH FUND SELECTION SYSTEM.
2: SEE TABLE 22 FOR A BRIEF DESCRIPTION OF THE TOP-PERFORMING MKTIME MODELS. THE MTM1 MODEL IS BUY & HOLD.
3.DURING THE LAST EIGHT (8) TRANSACTIONS.

In other words, the index outperformed System 42 during 82-86 by approximately 10%. During 87-91, System 42 outperformed the index by 10%. As a result, the system's 11-year performance was the same as the S&P 500 Index.

The percentage of Buy/Sell transactions that were profitable during the 1st and 2nd 5-year periods also differed as indicated below:

	PROFITABLE TRANSACTIONS	
Period	*Number*	*Percentage*
1982 - 1986	44	56%
1987 - 1991	55	69%
1982 - 1992	108	62%

■ SYSTEM 42 HAD SUBSTANTIALLY HIGHER TOTAL 5-YEAR **(88-92)** total returns than the index as indicated by the following comparisons:

MAR	22% vs. 16%
inflation-adjusted total return	110% vs. 60%
End-of-period inflation-adjusted market value of $1,000 lump sum investment	$2,100 vs. $1,600

"Risk" Performance Evaluation

Tables 51 A and B and 52 provide data for evaluating System 42 "risk" performance during the aforementioned 5-year periods, as shown below:

	5 - YEAR PERIOD	
Criteria	*1982 - 1986*	*1987 - 1991*
Maximum Transaction Loss	5.6%	7.8%
Minimum Percent Profitable Transactions	37.5%	37.5%

7: HOW TO SELECT YOUR MOST SUITABLE INVESTMENT SYSTEM

Introduction

In Chapter 6, we have presented the hypothetical performance of the five 1993 top-performing investment systems during the 11-year period from 1982 through 1992. In this chapter we provide comparative data to assist individual investors in selecting their most suitable investment system. The top-performing systems are compared on the basis of (1) their past performance and (2) their implementation requirements.

System Performance Comparison

Table 53 tabulates the annual and mean annualized returns (adjusted for trading fees) during the 11-year period of the five top-performing systems and the S&P 500 Index (SYS101). The table also indicates the year in which each system had a minimum annual return. Table 54 summarizes the hypothetical performance of the five systems and the index in accordance with the "return" and the "risk" performance criteria described in Chapter 2.

"Return" Performance Evaluation

Table 55 ranks the five systems by

(1) their mean annualized returns during the 11-year (88-92) periods and

(2) their average percentage of profitable transactions during the 11-year period.

Figure 16 represents a graphical picture of the system ranking by their mean annualized returns.

"Risk" Performance Evaluation

Table 56 ranks the five systems by (1) their minimum annual return; (2) their minimum percentage of profitable transactions;

TABLE 53
ANNUAL RETURNS ADJUSTED FOR TRADING FEES (%)
1993 TOP-PERFORMING INVESTMENT SYSTEMS; 11-YEAR PERIOD FROM 1982 THROUGH 1992

	INVESTMENT SYSTEM CONSISTING OF: GROWTH FUND OR GFSS (1) /MKTIME MODEL (2)					
YEAR	SYS101 SP 500/MTM1	SYS201 SP500/MTM2	SYS301 SP 500/MTM3	SYS42 GFSS2/MTM4	SYS52 GFSS2/MTM5	SYS62 GFSS2/MTM6
1982	21.6	21.6	28.1	24.2	46.3	52.5
1983	22.5	22.5	20.2	13.0	22.2	28.3
1984	6.2	6.2	10.2	4.2*	10.3*	13.0*
1985	31.8	31.8	31.8	5.8	35.7	35.4
1986	18.8	18.8	18.4	7.1	41.9	40.2
1987	5.2	36.0	33.4	24.8	27.7	39.5
1988	16.6	16.6	16.6	33.8	30.1	42.6
1989	31.7	31.7	28.8	23.6	40.9	50.7
1990	-3.1*	-3.1*	-0.5*	28.8	21.1	33.7
1991	30.5	30.5	25.4	16.0	61.8	72.0
1992	7.7	3.8	3.8	9.4	16.6	21.9
11-YR MAR (82-92)	16.7	19.0	19.2	17.0	31.5	38.3
5-YR MAR (88-92)	15.9	15.1	14.2	22.0	33.2	43.2

NOTES:

1. GFSS = GROWTH FUND SELECTION SYSTEM; SEE TABLE 32 FOR A BRIEF DESCRIPTION OF THE GFSS2 GROWTH FUND SELECTION SYSTEM.
2. SEE TABLE 22 FOR A BRIEF DESCRIPTION OF THE TOP-PERFORMING MKTIME MODELS.
3. * INDICATES MINIMUM ANNUAL RETURN DURING THE 11-YEAR PERIOD FROM 1982 THROUGH 1992.

TABLE 54
HYPOTHETICAL PERFORMANCE SUMMARY
1993 TOP-PERFORMING INVESTMENT SYSTEMS; 11-YEAR PERIOD FROM 1982 THROUGH 1992

A. "RETURN" PERFORMANCE CRITERIA (%)						
	INVESTMENT SYSTEM CONSISTING OF: GROWTH FUND OR GFSS (1) /MKTIME MODEL (2)					
PERFORMANCE CRITERION	**SYS101 SP 500/MT M1**	**SYS201 SP500/M TM2**	**SYS301 SP 500/MT M3**	**SYS42 GFSS2/ MTM4**	**SYS52 GFSS2/ MTM5**	**SYS62 GFSS2/ MTM6**
MEAN ANNUALIZED RETURN (MAR) (%)	16.7	19.0	19.2	17.0	31.5	38.3
AVERAGE % OF PROFITABLE BUY/SELL TRANSACTIONS (APT)	NA	NA	NA	62.0	80.0	77.0
MEAN TRANSACTION RETURN (MTR) (%)	NA	NA	NA	1.0	6.1	6.1
B. "RISK" PERFORMANCE CRITERIA (%)						
MINIMUM ANNUAL RETURN OR MAXIMUM ANNUAL LOSS (82-92)	-3.1	-3.1	-0.5	4.2	10.3	13.0
MINIMUM % OF PROFITABLE BUY/SELL TRANSACTIONS (MPT) (NOTE 3)	NA	NA	NA	25.0	62.5	62.5
MINIMUM TRANSACTION RETURN OR MAXIMUM TRANSACTION LOSS (MTL) (%)	NA	NA	NA	-7.8	-2.8	-3.3

NOTES:1: GFSS = GROWTH FUND SELECTION SYSTEM: SEE TABLE 32 FOR A BRIEF DESCRIPTION OF THE GFSS2 GROWTH FUND SELECTION SYSTEM.
2: SEE TABLE 22 FOR A BRIEF DESCRIPTION OF THE TOP-PERFORMING MKTIME MODELS. THE MTM1 MODEL IS BUY & HOLD.
3. DURING THE LAST EIGHT (8) TRANSACTIONS.

TABLE 55
1993 TOP-PERFORMING INVESTMENT SYSTEMS
RANKED BY THE "RETURN" PAST-PERFORMANCE CRITERIA
11-YEAR PERIOD FROM 1982 THROUGH 1992

	11-YEAR MAR		5-YEAR MAR		AVG % PROFITABLE TRANSACTIONS	
RANK	SYSTEM	MAR (%)	SYSTEM	MAR (%)	SYSTEM	AVG %
1	SYS62	38.3	SYS62	43.2	SYS52	80
2	SYS52	31.5	SYS52	33.2	SYS62	77
3	SYS301	19.2	SYS42	22.2	SYS42	62
4	SYS201	19.0	SYS201	15.1	SYS201	NA
5	SYS42	17.0	SYS301	14.2	SYS301	NA
BH	SYS101	16.7	SYS101	15.9	SYS101	NA

NOTES:
1. SEE TABLES 51 AND 54 FOR SYSTEM DEFINITIONS.

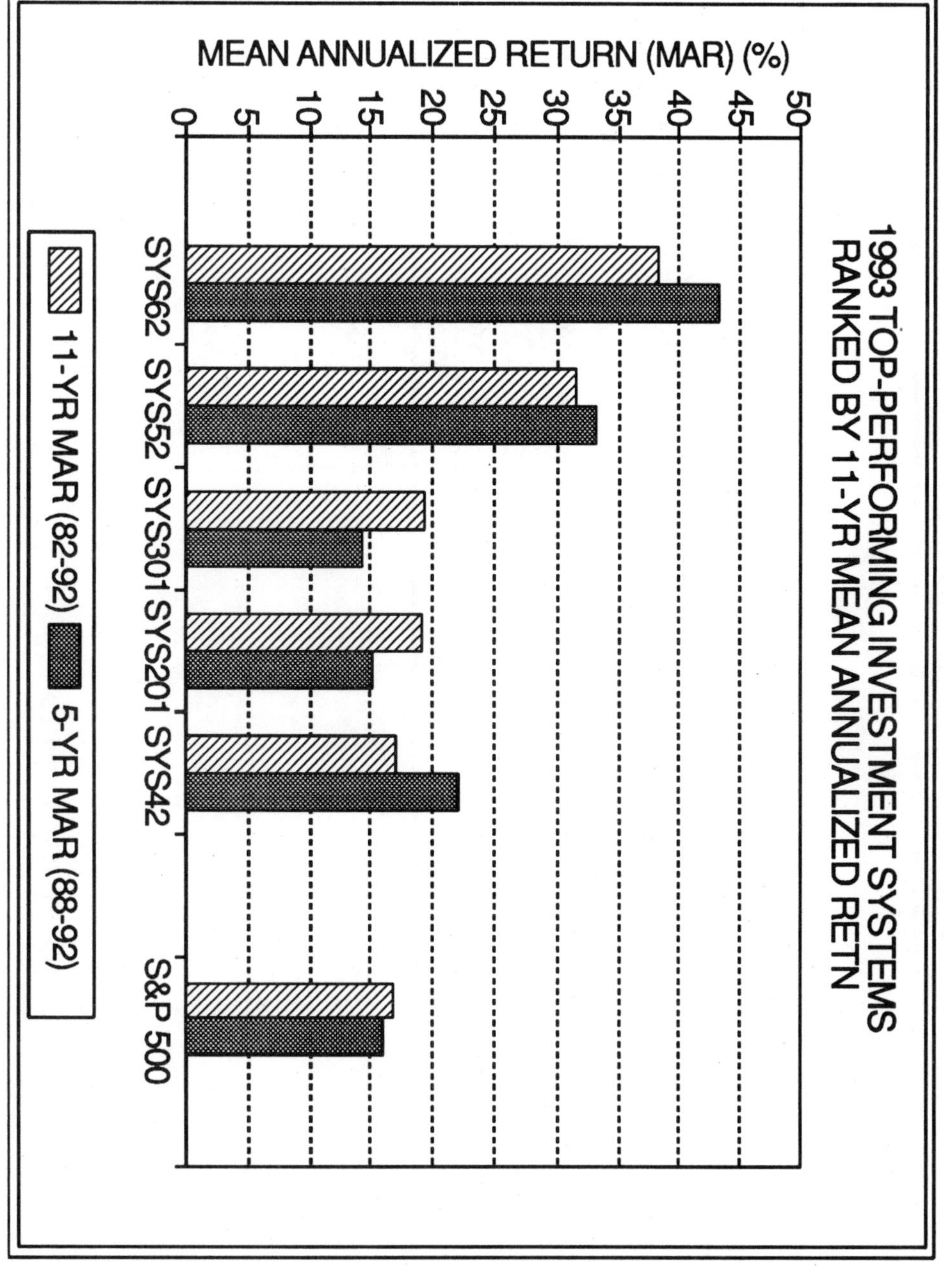
1993 TOP-PERFORMING INVESTMENT SYSTEMS
RANKED BY 11-YR MEAN ANNUALIZED RETN
MEAN ANNUALIZED RETURN (MAR) (%)
0
5
10
15
20
25
30
35
40
45
50
SYS62
SYS52
SYS301
SYS201
SYS42
S&P 500
11-YR MAR (82-92)
5-YR MAR (88-92)

FIGURE 16

TABLE 56
1993 TOP-PERFORMING INVESTMENT SYSTEMS
RANKED BY THE "RISK" PAST-PERFORMANCE CRITERIA
11-YEAR PERIOD FROM 1982 THROUGH 1992

	MINIMUM ANNUAL RTN		MINIMUM % PROFITABLE TRANSACTIONS		MAXIMUM TRANSACTION LOSS (%)	
RANK	SYSTEM	RTN (%)	SYSTEM	MIN(%)	SYSTEM	MAX LOSS
1	SYS62	13.0	SYS62	62.5	SYS52	2.8
2	SYS52	10.3	SYS52	62.5	SYS62	3.3
3	SYS42	4.2	SYS42	25.0	SYS42	7.8
4	SYS301	-0.5	SYS301	NA	SYS301	NA
5	SYS201	-3.1	SYS201	NA	SYS201	NA
BH	SYS101	-3.1	SYS101	NA	SYS101	NA

NOTES:
1. SEE TABLES 51 AND 54 FOR SYSTEM DEFINITIONS.

and (3) their maximum transaction loss during the 11-year period. Figure 17 presents a graphical picture of the system ranking by their minimum annual returns.

System Performance Summary

The above tables and figures indicate that:

- SYSTEM 62 HAD THE HIGHEST "RETURN" PERFORMANCE WITH MEAN ANNUALIZED RETURNS OF 38% AND 43% DURING THE 11-YEAR AND 5-YEAR PERIODS, RESPECTIVELY.
- Systems 62 and 52 had the best "risk" performance with comparable values of minimum annual return; minimum percentage of profitable transactions and maximum transaction loss.

System Implementation Comparison

Chapter 8 describes and compares three methods of implementing or executing mutual fund investment systems:

(1) do-it-yourself;
(2) newsletter/hotline service; and
(3) investment advisory service.

Table 57 compares the do-it-yourself implementation requirements for the 1993 top-performing investment systems. Three types of implementation requirements are shown, as follows:

- DATA INPUT FREQUENCY indicating how often data is required to be recorded or inputted into a personal computer.
- SOFTWARE REQUIREMENTS indicating what types of software are required for use with your personal computer. Two types of software are indicated: (1) commercially available mktime/spreadsheet software and (2) spreadsheets to be prepared using the indicators and rules described in this report.
- TRADES PER YEAR indicating how many fund transfers are executed each year.

Table 58 and Figure 18 show the number of trades executed each year and the average number of trades per year for each system.

FIGURE 17

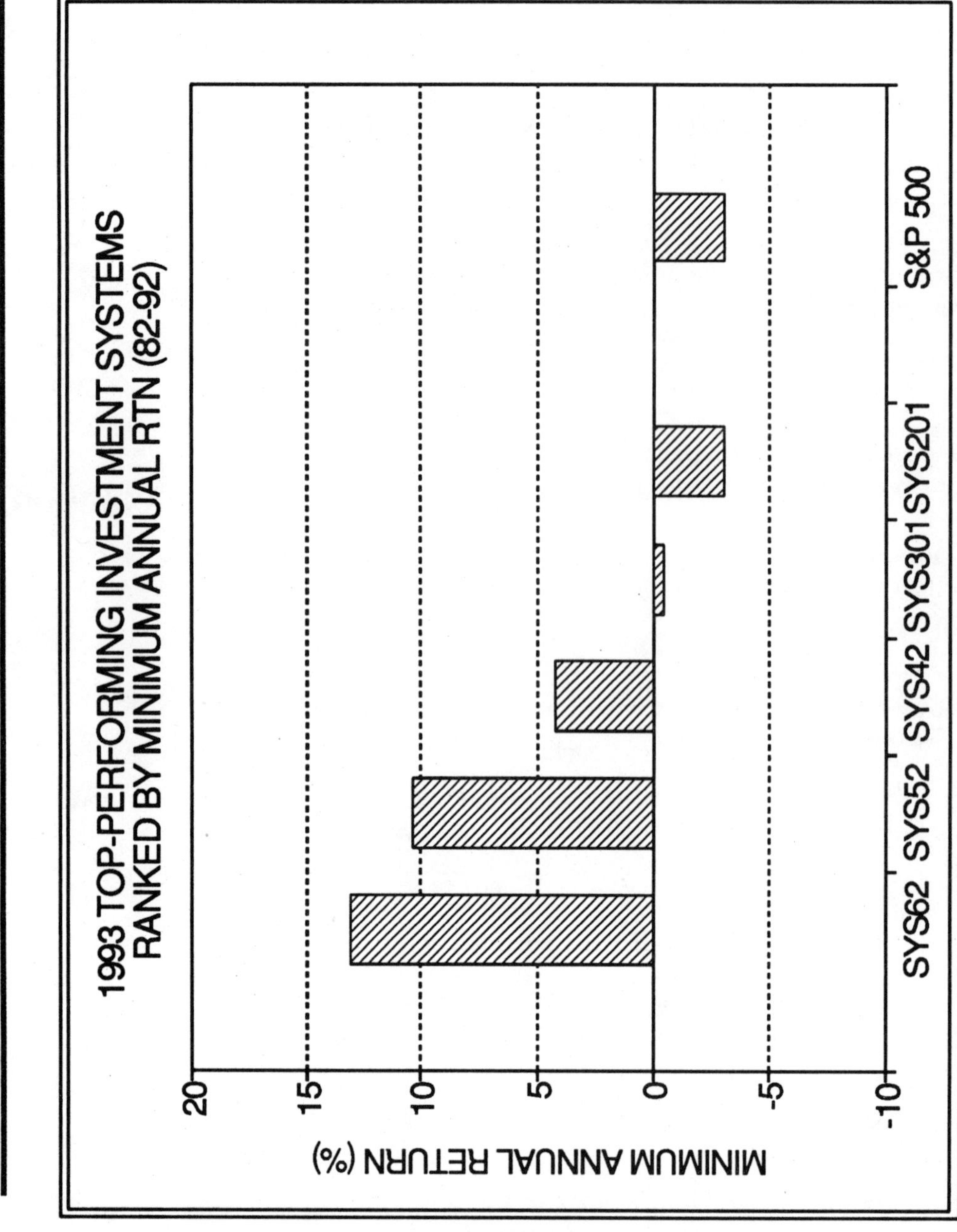
1993 TOP-PERFORMING INVESTMENT SYSTEMS
RANKED BY MINIMUM ANNUAL RTN (82-92)
MINIMUM ANNUAL RETURN (%)
20
15
10
5
0
-5
-10
SYS62
SYS52
SYS42
SYS301
SYS201
S&P 500

TABLE 57
1993 TOP-PERFORMING INVESTMENT SYSTEMS
DO-IT-YOURSELF IMPLEMENTATION REQUIREMENTS

		SOFTWARE REQUIREMENTS		
SYSTEM	**DATA INPUT FREQUENCY**	**MKTIME MODEL**	**GTH FUND SELECTION**	**AVG # TRADES PER YEAR (NOTE 4)**
SYS201	WEEKLY	NONE	NONE	0.2
SYS301	WEEKLY	YES (1)	YES (1)	0.8
SYS42	NONE	NONE	NONE	31.6
SYS52	DAILY	YES (2)	YES (3)	9.2
SYS62	DAILY	YES (2)	YES (3)	12.0

NOTES:

1. VIA SPREADSHEETS WHICH IMPLEMENT THE MKTIME INDICATORS AND RULES DESCRIBED IN APPENDIX C.
2.VIA COMMERCIALLY AVAILABLE MARKET TIMING SOFTWARE DESCRIBED IN APPENDIX E.
3.VIA SPREADSHEETS WHICH IMPLEMENT THE GROWTH FUND SELECTION INDICATORS AND RULES DESCRIBED IN SECTION 5.
4. DURING THE 5-YEAR PERIOD (88-92).

TABLE 58
1993 TOP-PERFORMING INVESTMENT SYSTEMS; # ASSET SWITCHES PER YEAR 11-YEAR PERIOD FROM 1982 THROUGH 1992

	INVESTMENT SYSTEM CONSISTING OF: GROWTH FUND OR GFSS (1) /MKTIME MODEL (2)					
YEAR	SYS101 SP 500/MTM1	SYS201 SP500/MTM2	SYS301 SP 500/MTM3	SYS42 GFSS2/MTM4	SYS52 GFSS2/MTM5	SYS62 GFSS2/MTM6
1982	0	0	1.0	30	6	6
1983	0	0	0.5	30	8	10
1984	0	0	1.5	34	4	4
1985	0	0	0	30	6	12
1986	0	0	0.3	30	11	16
1987	0	2.0	1.7	34	12	12
1988	0	0	0	30	8	12
1989	0	0	0.5	32	11	14
1990	0	0	1.0	34	11	11
1991	0	0	1.7	30	7	9
1992	0	1	1.0	32	9	14
AVG # SWITCHES 11-YR	0	0.3	0.8	31.5	8.5	10.9
AVG # SWITCHES 5-YR	0	0.2	0.8	31.6	9.2	12.0

NOTES:
1. GFSS = GROWTH FUND SELECTION SYSTEM; SEE TABLE 32 FOR A BRIEF DESCRIPTION OF THE GFSS2 GROWTH FUND SELECTION SYSTEM.
2. SEE TABLE 22 FOR A BRIEF DESCRIPTION OF THE TOP-PERFORMING MKTIME MODELS.
3. SYS301 MAKES PARTIAL TRANSFERS OF ASSETS FROM GROWTH TO MONEY MARKET MUTUAL FUNDS.

FIGURE 18

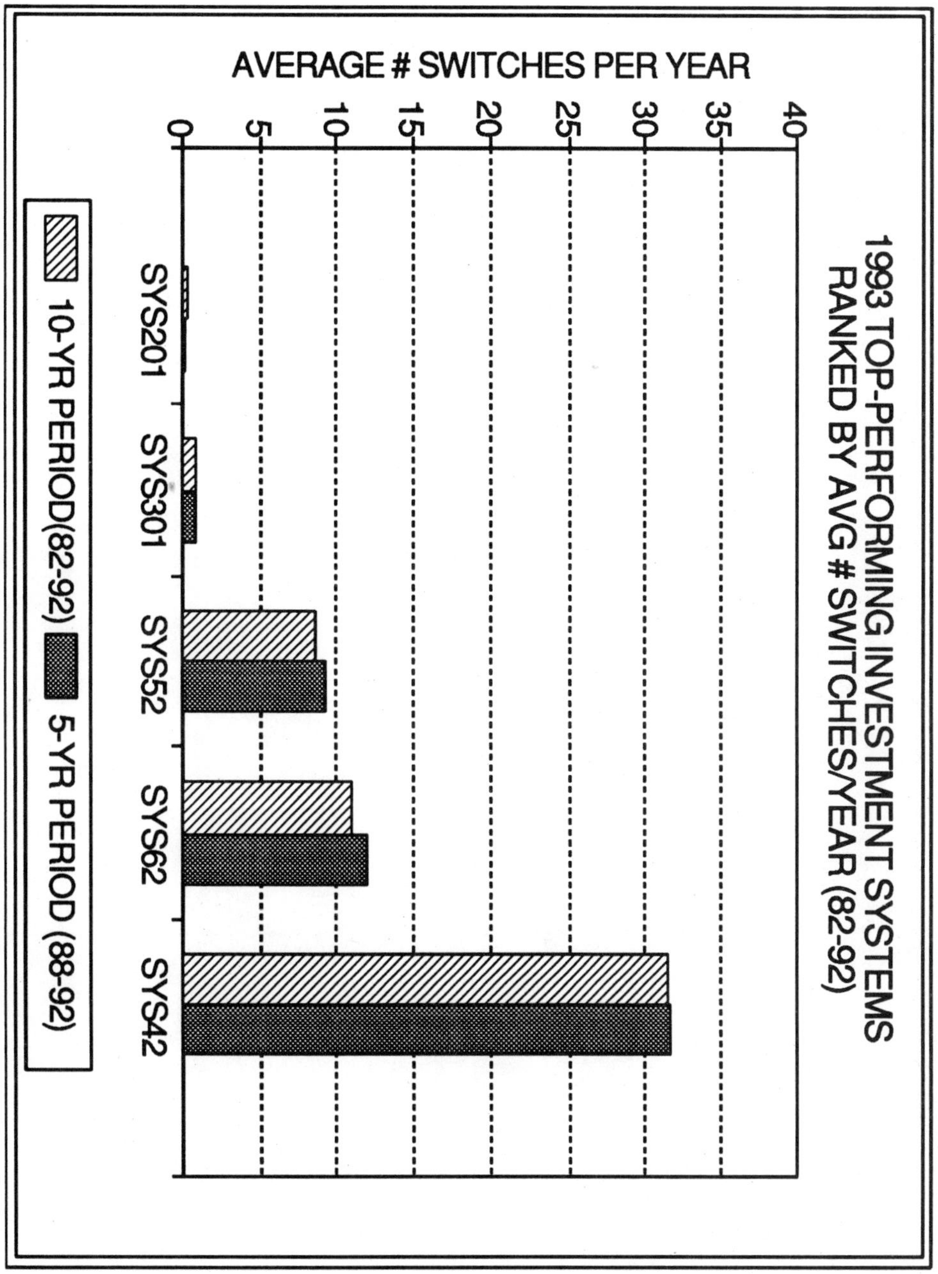

1993 TOP-PERFORMING INVESTMENT SYSTEMS
RANKED BY AVG # SWITCHES/YEAR (82-92)

AVERAGE # SWITCHES PER YEAR

0
5
10
15
20
25
30
35
40

SYS201
SYS301
SYS52
SYS62
SYS42

10-YR PERIOD(82-92)
5-YR PERIOD (88-92)

System Selection Summary

To obtain the highest investment performance with minimum risk, an individual investor should employ the top-performing System 62 or System 52.

To implement these systems on a do-it-yourself basis, an individual investor should be:

Computer literate with commercially available market timing software and spreadsheet software

Willing and able to input data on a daily basis

Willing and able to execute trades on a daily basis at a rate of 10 to 12 times per year

Individual investors (who are not computer literate or are not willing or able to input and/or execute trades on a daily basis) can still implement the top-performing system(s) using the methods discussed in Chapter 8.

8: HOW TO IMPLEMENT YOUR SELECTED SYSTEM

Introduction

We recognize that many readers wish to perform a "hands-on" implementation of the top-performing systems described in this book. Such readers will have the required computer literacy plus the time and motivation to successfully implement these systems. However, there are probably many other readers who do not possess the required computer literacy or do not have the time required and associated motivation to "do-it-yourself." To accommodate such readers who may desire to invest using the top-performing AMFI systems, we have encouraged other non-AMFI organizations to provide alternate methods for implementing the AMFI top-performing investment systems. **However, the authors do not and cannot assume any responsibility for the investment performance of such organizations.**

Table 20 (page 60) outlines four alternate methods for implementing your selected, top-performing mutual fund investment system. These methods are as follows:

- Do-it-yourself
- Subscribe to a non-AMFI hotline service and associated newsletter
- Hire a registered investment adviser who faithfully implements the AMFI top-performing systems
- Form an investment club that uses any one of the above methods

In this chapter, we describe the tasks to be performed when employing the first three implementation methods; then, we compare their annual costs; and, finally, we describe several ground rules which should be followed to help ensure that your actual investment performance matches the AMFI published performance.

Investment Implementation Tasks

Table 59 lists the tasks to be performed in order to implement each of the three alternate investment system implementation methods. These tasks are grouped under four major headings:

- Initial setup
- Daily tasks
- Execution tasks
- File maintenance tasks

Initial setup under the do-it-yourself implementation involves

(1) the purchase and installation of a personal computer and associated market timing (mktime) software and

(2) the purchase and installation of spreadsheet software and the growth fund selection spreadsheet.

Initial setup under the hotline implementation requires only a subscription to a non-AMFI newsletter and associated hotline service. Initial setup under the investment advisory implementation requires only the execution of an asset management agreement with an appropriate registered investment adviser.

On each trading day, the investor using the do-it-yourself method inputs previous-day market data (either manually or via a wire service) and observes the resulting mktime status and associated growth fund selection. The investor using the hotline service obtains the same information by telephone from a recording. The investor using an advisory service has no daily tasks to perform.

When a Buy or Sell signal is generated, the investors using the do-it-yourself and hotline methods telephone their mutual fund trading broker and request that assets be switched accordingly. The investor using an advisory service has no execution tasks to perform.

The investor performs file maintenance tasks under all three implementation methods.

Investment Implementation Costs

Tables 60 A, B, and C indicate the formulas for computing the annual cost of the three investment implementation methods for three types of investment accounts:
(1) accounts under $50,000;
(2) accounts between $50,000 and $100,000; and
(3) accounts between $100,000 and $250,000.

TABLE 59: INVESTMENT SYSTEMS IMPLEMENTATION TASKS VS METHODS

TASK #	IMPLEMENTATION TASK	IMPLEMENTATION METHOD		
		DO-IT-YOURSELF	HOTLINE SERVICE	INVESTMENT ADVISOR
1	INITIAL SETUP			
1a	Purchase and install personal computer if needed	X		
1b	Purchase and install mktime software on your computer	X		
1c	Purchase and install spreadsheet on your computer	X		
1d	Develop & install growth fund selection system spreadsheet	X		
1e	Subscribe to hotline service		X	
1f	Execute an asset management agreement with an appropriate investment advisor			X
2	DAILY TASKS			
2a	Input data for mktime software program via telephone or manually & determine mktime status	X		
2b	Input data manually for growth fund selection system spreadsheet & determine top-performing growth fund	X		
2c	Telephone hotline recording to obtain and to record the mktime signals [if any] & associated growth fund selection		X	
3	SIGNAL EXECUTION TASKS			
3a	When a Buy signal is generated, call your mutual fund trading broker to transfer assets from a money market fund to the selected growth fund(s)	X	X	
3b	When a Sell signal is generated, call your mutual fund trading broker to transfer assets from previously selected growth fund(s) to a money market fund	X	X	
4	FILE MAINTENANCE TASKS			
4a	File transaction or trade statements when received	X	X	X
4b	File quarterly account statements when received	X	X	X

Four types of implementation costs are shown:

- Data input cost via telephone transmission or via manual input from the *Wall Street Journal*
- Hotline subscription cost
- Mutual fund trading fees
- Investment adviser management fees

The total cost column contains the formulas for the annual total cost of each implementation method as a function of the amount (A) switched from one mutual fund to another. The "do-it-yourself" implementation costs do NOT include the costs of purchase and maintenance or support of a personal computer and the required software. Table 60D and Figure 19 show how the total implementation cost for each implementation method varies with the average amount switched in each of the 11 one-way switches. The table and figure show that the total cost (as a percentage of the account value) varies as follows:

METHOD	$10K ACCOUNT	$250K ACCOUNT
Do-It-Yourself	6.2%	1.3%
Hotline Service	6.2%	1.3%
Investment Advisor	7.3%	2.1%

Implementation problem areas

We have been employing the top-performing, software-driven investment systems for approximately 30 months. During this period, we have encountered two major problems as listed below.

- INCORRECT INPUT DATA To the mktime software when using manual input and when using telephone transmission. Manual input is subject to the usual human transcription errors. Wire service data transmitted during the evening after the market closing is often tentative and subject to revision in the early morning of the next day. The use of both types of data input as a cross-check will reduce the data input errors substantially.
- INABILITY TO FOLLOW SYSTEM-GENERATED SIGNALS. It is often very difficult to implement the system-generated signals when the market is moving in a direction opposite to the signal-generated direction. Yet experience has shown that deviations from the system signals usually (but not always) end in losses or lost opportunities.

TABLE 60A
ANNUAL COST FORMULAS
ALTERNATE INVESTMENT SYSTEM IMPLEMENTATION METHODS
ACCOUNTS UNDER $50,000

	ANNUAL COSTS ($)				
IMPLEMENTATION METHOD	DATA INPUT [1]	HOTLINE SERVICE [2]	TRADING FEES [3]	MGMT FEE [4]	TOTAL FEE [5]
1. DO-IT-YOURSELF	$180	–	11X ($20 + .002A)	–	$400 + .022A (NOTE 6)
2. HOTLINE SERVICE	–	$180	11X ($20 + .002A)	–	$400 + .022A
3. INVESTMENT ADVISOR	–	–	11X ($20 + .001A)	.018A	$220 + .029A

NOTES:
1. DATA INPUT COST IS THE ANNUAL COST OF OBTAINING DAILY SOFTWARE INPUT DATA VIA TELEPHONE OR MANUALLY USING THE WALL STREET JOURNAL. THE ANNUAL COST FOR EITHER APPROACH IS ABOUT THE SAME.
2. THE HOTLINE SERVICE WOULD PROVIDE DAILY MKTIME SIGNALS AND ASSOCIATED GROWTH FUND SELECTION(S) FROM A RECORDING VIA TELEPHONE.
3. MUTUAL FUND TRADING FEES SHOWN ARE BASED UPON BROKERAGE ACCOUNTS WITH JACK WHITE & CO. [FOR METHODS 1 &2] AND WITH SHAREHOLDER SERVICES CORP. [FOR METHOD 3]. ANNUAL FEES ARE BASED UPON AN AVERAGE OF 11 ONE-WAY SWITCHES PER YEAR AND THE FEE SCHEDULES SHOWN IN APPENDIX G.
4. THE MANAGEMENT FEE SHOWN IS BASED UPON THE FOLLOWING SCHEDULE: (1) 1.8% OF INVESTED ASSETS FOR THE 1ST $100,000; (2) 1.0% FOR THE NEXT $150,000; AND 0.8% THEREAFTER. A MINIMUM FEE OF $400 PER YEAR IS CHARGED.
5. A EQUALS THE AMOUNT OF ASSETS IN AN ACCOUNT THAT ARE SWITCHED FROM ONE MUTUAL FUND TO ANOTHER.
6. DO-IT-YOURSELF COSTS DO NOT INCLUDE THE COSTS OF PERSONAL COMPUTER PURCHASE AND MAINTENANCE AND OF REQUIRED SOFTWARE.

TABLE 60 (CONTINUED): ANNUAL COST FORMULAS ALTERNATE INVESTMENT SYSTEM IMPLEMENTATION METHODS

IMPLEMENTATION METHOD	ANNUAL COSTS ($) DATA INPUT [1]	HOTLINE SERVICE [2]	TRADING FEES [3]	MGMT FEE [4]	TOTAL FEE [5]
B. ACCOUNTS FROM $50,000 TO $100,000					
1. DO-IT-YOURSELF	$180	–	11X ($35 + .001A)	–	$565 + .011A (NOTE 6)
2. HOTLINE SERVICE	–	$180	11X ($35 + .001A)	–	$565 + .011A
3. INVESTMENT ADVISOR	–	–	11X ($35 + .0005A)	.018A	$385 + .0235A
C. ACCOUNTS FROM $50,000 TO $100,000					
1. DO-IT-YOURSELF	$180	–	11X ($35 + .001A)	–	$565 + .011A (NOTE 6)
2. HOTLINE SERVICE	–	$180	11X ($35 + .001A)	–	$565 + .011A
3. INVESTMENT ADVISOR	–	–	11X ($35 + .0005A)	$1800+ .01X (A-$100K)	$385 + .0235A

TABLE 60D
ANNUAL COSTS OF ALTERNATE INVESTMENT SYSTEM IMPLEMENTATIONS VS ACCOUNT MARKET VALUE

	INVESTMENT SYSTEM IMPLEMENTATION METHOD					
	DO-IT-YOURSELF		HOTLINE SERVICE		INVESTMENT ADVISER	
ACCOUNT MARKET VALUE ($000)	ANNUAL COST	% ACCT VALUE	ANNUAL COST	% ACCT VALUE	ANNUAL COST	% ACCT VALUE
10	620	6.2	620	6.2	730	7.3
20	840	4.2	840	4.2	840	4.2
30	1060	3.5	1060	3.5	1090	3.6
40	1280	3.2	1280	3.2	1380	3.5
50	1120	2.2	1120	2.2	1560	3.1
100	1670	1.7	1670	1.7	2740	2.7
150	2220	1.5	2220	1.5	3690	2.5
200	2770	1.4	2770	1.4	4470	2.2
250	3320	1.3	3320	1.3	5240	2.1

INVESTMENT SYSTEM IMPLEMENTATION
ANNUAL COST (%) VS ACCOUNT VALUE
ANNUAL COST (% OF ACCT VALUE)
0
0.5
1
1.5
2
2.5
3
3.5
4
4.5
5
5.5
6
6.5
7
7.5
8
10
20
30
40
50
100
150
200
250
ACCOUNT VALUE ($000)
DO-IT-YOURSELF
HOTLINE SERVICE
INVEST. ADVISER

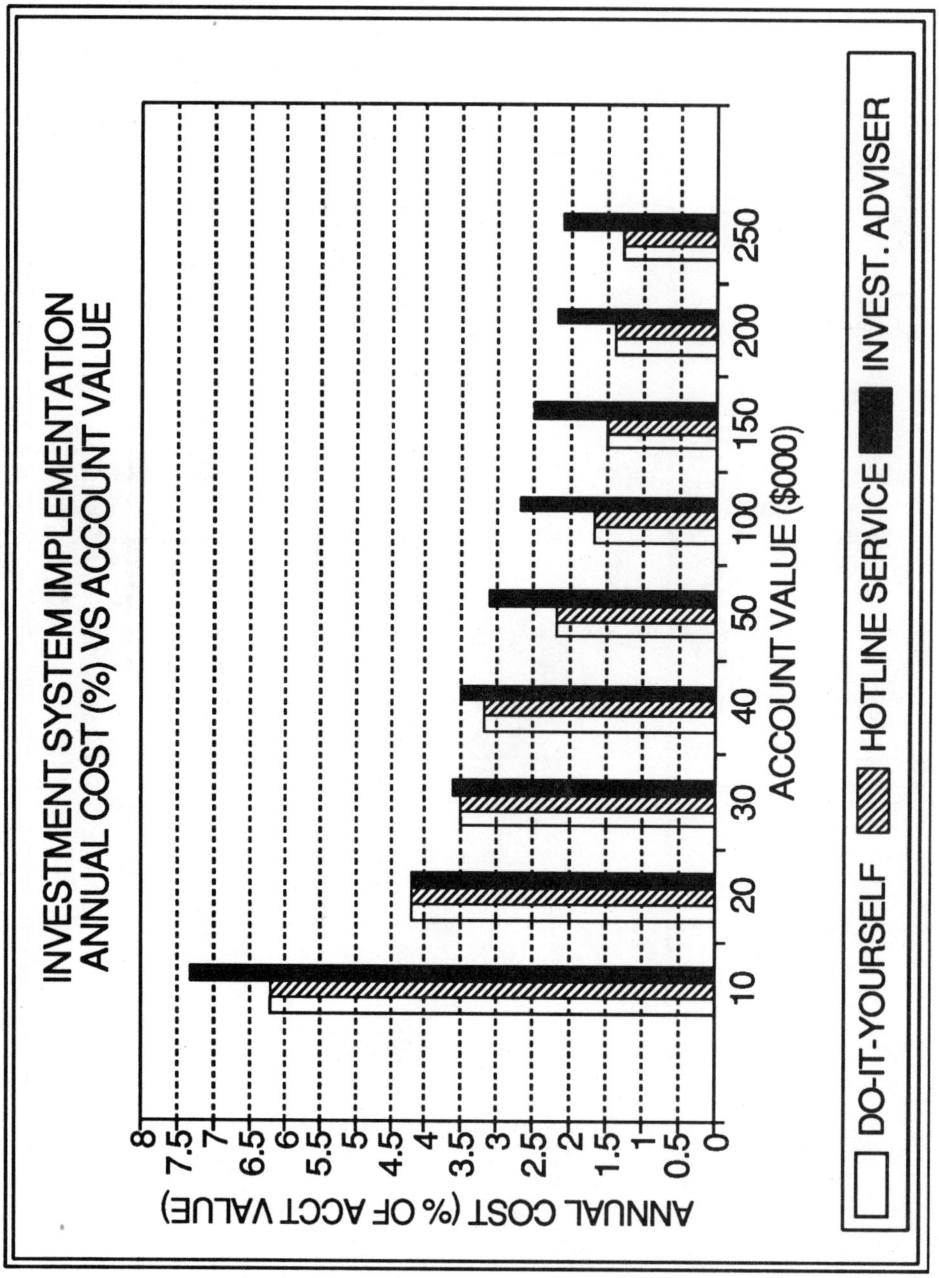

Figure 19

9: HOW TO GET STARTED

Introduction

In the preceding chapters of this book, we have presented:

- A systematic methodology for investing in mutual funds
- The hypothetical performance of five top-performing systems (developed with this methodology) during the 11-year period from 1982 through 1992. The top two systems achieved mean annualized returns or compounded rates of return of 38% and 32%, respectively.

How can an individual investor benefit from the material presented in this book? In the following paragraphs, we answer this question.

Step 1: Join and Participate in AMFI

As an AMFI member, you will receive six bimonthly newsletters (or meeting notes) each year. This newsletter (approximately 30 to 40 pages long) reports upon the results of the mutual fund investment research conducted by individual AMFI members. At the end of each year, you will also receive the AMFI special report (an updated version of this book) if you renew your membership within 30 days after the AMFI letter solicitation is mailed.

Six bimonthly regular meetings and three special meetings are conducted by each AMFI chapter (currently Philadelphia and Detroit). Slides from the latest newsletter are presented at each regular bimonthly meeting to explain the research results and to stimulate member discussion and interaction. At the three special meetings, a mutual fund investment course is conducted using the latest AMFI special report as a text.

We will establish and support AMFI chapters in other regions of the country where there are at least ten AMFI members. Such chapters will be able to conduct the same AMFI meetings as are currently conducted by the Philadelphia and Detroit chapters.

Write AMFI for an application or additional information. AMFI has an advertisement in the back of this book.

Step 2: Investing In AMFI Systems

As indicated in Chapter 1, AMFI, the authors, and the publisher do not make any investment recommendations nor assume any responsibility for the accuracy of the information presented in this book.

Neither are there any claim[s] nor implications that historical or hypothetical performance data necessarily have any relevance to the future performance of the overall market, individual mutual funds or mutual fund investment systems.

However, in this book, we have described each investment system in sufficient detail so that an individual investor or a registered investment adviser can:

- Test and evaluate each investment system
- Implement and/or execute each investment system on a continuing basis

In Chapter 8 of this book, we described and compared three methods for implementing and executing the top-performing investment systems:

(1) do-it-yourself;

(2) use a hotline service; or

(3) hire a registered investment adviser.

We have tried to provide the required information to individual investors desiring to use the first method. The authors will also do the following, for AMFI members, who wish to use the second and third investment system implementation methods:

- Furnish the name, address and telephone number of non-AMFI organizations who will provide either hotline service or investment advisory services.
- Assist any AMFI members who wish to provide either the hotline service or the investment advisory service discussed in Chapter 8.

APPENDIX A: GLOSSARY

AMERICAN ASSOCIATION OF INDIVIDUAL INVESTORS (AAII): An independent, nonprofit corporation which educates individual investors regarding a wide range of investment vehicles.

ANNUAL RETURN: The increase or decrease in market value of a security during a calendar year.

ASSOCIATION OF MUTUAL FUND INVESTORS (AMFI): An independent, nonprofit corporation which educates individual investors regarding mutual funds by conducting programs of research, education and information dissemination.

BALANCED MUTUAL FUND: A mutual fund (usually open-end) that invests in both common stocks and bonds and often in preferred stock.

BARRONS': A weekly publication by Dow-Jones providing financial news and views.

BETA: A measure of investment risk which compares the volatility of a security with respect to the volatility of the overall stock market as represented by the S&P 500 Index.

BLUE CHIP STOCKS: Stocks of an investment-grade of the highest standing.

BOND: A security that represents a loan by the investor to a corporation, municipality, state or federal government. It is expressed in terms of a specified face value, interest rate and date of maturity when the loan will be repaid.

BROKER: An agent who buys and sells securities and commodities for the public for a sales commission.

BUY SIGNAL: A signal (generated by a mktime model) indicating that assets should be invested in stocks or growth funds.

BUY/SELL TRANSACTION: An investment transaction that begins when a Buy signal is generated and ends when the next Buy signal is generated. It includes a Buy period (when assets are invested in a growth fund) and a Sell period (when assets are invested in a money market fund).

CAPITAL GAINS OR LOSSES: The profit or loss resulting from the purchase and subsequent sale of a security or mutual fund.

CERTIFICATE OF DEPOSIT (CD): A document that represents a loan by the investor to a bank and is expressed in terms of a specified face value, interest rate and date of maturity when the loan will be repaid. At the present time (January 1993), these certificates are insured by the federal government for amounts up to $100,000.

CLOSED-END MUTUAL FUNDS: Closed-end funds operate with a fixed number of shares. The shares are not bought or sold from and to the fund. Instead, the shares are traded among individuals in a secondary market (i.e. a stock exchange) in the same manner as common stocks.

COMMON STOCK: Securities which represent an ownership interest in a corporation.

DOW-JONES INDUSTRIAL AVERAGE (DJIA): A benchmark stock average of 30 blue chip industrial stocks selected for total market value and broad public ownership.

EQUITY SECURITIES: Same as common stock.

GROWTH FUND: A mutual fund that seeks to maximize its return through capital gains. It typically invests in stocks that are expected to increase in value faster than inflation.

GROWTH FUND SELECTION SYSTEM: A precisely defined methodology to determine the best growth fund for investment when a mktime model generates a Buy signal.

HULBERT FINANCIAL DIGEST: A newsletter which evaluates the past performance of newsletters which provide investment advice.

HYPOTHETICAL PERFORMANCE DATA: Investment performance data obtained by computer back-testing rather than actual investments. Computer back-testing of a precisely defined investment system consists of the simulation of the system's performance during a previous time period and the measurement of the system's performance during the period.

INDEX: A collection of a number of individual stocks. The index value is computed as an average of the daily prices or market value of the stocks and is used as a benchmark for investment performance.

INDEX MUTUAL FUND: A mutual fund (usually open-end) that invests in the same securities as those that are included within a major market index such as the S&P 500 Index.

INVESTMENT ADVISER: An individual or company which provides investment advisory and supervisory services for a fee.

INVESTMENT CLUB. A group of individuals who pool their assets and their knowledge in order to invest in stocks and/or mutual funds.

INVESTMENT RISK: The probability that the future return from an investment will differ from its expected value.

LOAD MUTUAL FUNDS: Mutual funds that charge a sales commission (called a load) when shares are purchased and/or a redemption (or exit) fee when shares are redeemed.

LONG-TERM PERFORMANCE RATING (LPR): A means of rating the past performance of mktime models and mutual fund investment systems during a 5-year period. It is defined as the mean of the 5-year and 2-year mean annualized returns.

MARKET TIMING (MKTIME) MODEL: A precisely defined methodology that determines when to buy stocks or growth mutual funds and when to sell such stocks or growth mutual funds.

MEAN ANNUALIZED RETURN (MAR): Used to measure the performance of a stock or growth fund with fluctuating annual returns over a period of two or more years. It is the mean value of the annual returns of a stock or growth fund over a specified number of years.

MONEY MARKET FUND: A mutual fund that invests in high-yield, short-term money market instruments such as U.S. T-bills and commercial paper.

MONIRESEARCH NEWSLETTER: A newsletter which evaluates the past performance of professional money managers who employ market timing.

MOVING AVERAGE: At a given date, the arithmetic average of prices for a security (or other financial data) during a fixed time period preceding and including the given date.

MUTUAL FUND: A company that pools the investments of many individuals and uses its capital to invest in the stock of many other companies.

MUTUAL FUND INVESTMENT SYSTEM: A precisely defined methodology for investing in mutual funds.

MUTUAL FUND TRADING BROKER: An agent who buys and sells many mutual funds for a transaction fee.

NASDAQ INDICES: Measures of the current price behavior of securities sold in the OTC (Over-the-Counter) stock market.

NATIONAL ASSOCIATION OF INVESTMENT CORPORATIONS (NAIC): A member-owned and operated organization which provides stock investment education for individual investors and investment clubs.

NET ASSET VALUE (NAV): Net asset value per share (NAV) is equal to the net worth (assets minus liabilities) of a fund divided by the number of outstanding shares.

NO-LOAD MUTUAL FUND: Mutual funds that do not charge a sales commission when shares are purchased nor a redemption fee when shares are sold.

OPEN END MUTUAL FUNDS: Investors buy and sell shares from and to an open-end fund. The fund offers to sell and redeem shares on a continual basis for an indefinite period. Therefore, the number of outstanding shares is constantly changing. Shares are purchased at the net asset value (NAV) plus sales commission (if any) and are redeemed at NAV less a redemption fee (if any).

OVER-THE-COUNTER (OTC): A securities market characterized by trading through broker-dealers via telephone rather than using the facilities of a stock exchange. Stocks of many small emerging growth companies are included in this market.

OVER-THE-COUNTER INDUSTRIAL (OTCI) INDEX: An index comprised of OTC industrial stocks.

PREFERRED STOCK: Securities which represent an ownership interest in a corporation and which have a prior claim (over common stock) on dividends and, in the event of liquidation, on assets.

REGISTERED INVESTMENT ADVISER: An investment adviser who is registered with the U.S. Securities and Exchange Commission (SEC). Such an adviser may also be registered with one or more state securities commissions.

RETURN OR TOTAL RETURN: The increase or decrease in market value of security during a specified time period. It is expressed in terms of percentage change or as a ratio of end-of-period value to start-of-period value.

S&P 500 INDEX: An index based upon the 500 largest stocks in the New York Stock Exchange. The index value is based upon the average of the market value of the component stocks. The index is used as a standard of investment performance.

SECTOR FUND: A mutual fund (usually open-end) that invests in a portfolio of common stocks covering one or two fields or industries such as health science, technology, leisure, etc.

SECURITY: Represents investment vehicles such as stocks, bonds, mutual funds, etc.

SELL SIGNAL: A signal (generated by a mktime model) indicating that shares of a stock or growth fund should be sold and that proceeds should be invested in a money market fund.

STANDARD & POOR'S CORPORATION (S&P): A company which publishes a variety of financial and investment reports and services.

STANDARD DEVIATION: A measure of investment risk based upon the fluctuation in the return of a security with respect to the expected return over a specified time period: namely, its mean annualized return during the past five or more years.

T-BILL: A short-term (3 months, 6 months or 12 months) security issued by the U.S. Treasury.

VOLATILITY: The degree of fluctuation in the market value of a security.

APPENDIX B: MKTIME MODEL MTM2 (S&P 500 DIVIDEND YIELD)

INTRODUCTION

One of the best indicators of major stock market tops and bottoms is the dividend yield of the S&P 500 Index. This yield is equal to the cash dividends paid out annually by the 500 stocks which comprise the index and is expressed as a percentage of the index.

Historically, the S&P 500 dividend yield has averaged 4.8%. Data provided by the Institute of Econometric Research (in their *Mutual Fund Forecaster* newsletter) and indicated in Table 61 shows the relationship between the dividend yield and major stock market declines.

Table 61 indicates that a major stock market decline usually follows within 12 to 24 months after the dividend yield falls below 3%.

MKTIME MODEL MTM2 DESCRIPTION

This mktime model employs the S&P 500 dividend yield as its sole mktime indicator in accordance with the followin rules:

When the current mktime status is Buy (i.e. invested in the stock market or in a growth fund), a Sell signal is generated when the S&P 500 dividend yield falls and remains below 3% for two weeks.

When the current mktime status is Sell (i.e. invested in a money market fund or cash equivalent), a Buy signal is generated when the S&P 500 dividend yield rises above 3.5%.

MTM2 PERFORMANCE RESULTS

During the 11-year period from 1982 through 1992, the MTM2 mktime model generated only two Sell signals in March 1987 and in January 1992. In 1987, a Buy signal was generated at the end of October one week after the "crash" on October 19th. No Buy signal has been generated as of January 1993 since the Sell signal in January 1992. The 1987 and 1992 annual returns for the S&P 500 Index when MTM2-timed and when bought and held are shown below:

S&P 500 INDEX ANNUAL RETURNS		
	ANNUAL RETURNS %	
YEAR	BUY/HOLD	MTM2-TIMED
1987	5.2	36.0
1992	7.7	3.8

In the other nine years of the 11-year period, the MTM2-timed system had the same annual returns as the S&P 500 Index when bought and held. **When timed by the MTM2 mktime model, the index achieved an 11-year MAR of 19% as compared to 16.7% for Buy/Hold. (See Table 49).**

MTM2 MKTIME MODEL IMPLEMENTATION

Barrons' weekly magazine publishes the S&P 500 dividend yield in every issue. This magazine is available on newsstands and in public libraries. An investor should record the dividend yields every week. When the yield is below 3% for two weeks, the investor should transfer assets from growth to money market funds. When the yield rises above 3.5%, the investor should transfer assets to a growth fund.

TABLE 61
S&P 500 DIVIDEND YIELD AS A MARKET TIMING INDICATOR
FUTURE MARKET PERFORMANCE VS S&P 500 DIVIDEND YIELD [1]
41-YEAR PERIOD FROM 1946 TO 1987

S&P 500 DIVIDEND YIELD	FUTURE STOCK MARKET PERFORMANCE (%)			
	6 MONTHS	12 MONTHS	24 MONTHS	36 MONTHS
BELOW 3%	-1	-5	-10	-1
3% TO 4%	1	4	9	10
4% TO 5%	7	14	21	26
5% TO 6%	4	11	33	56
6% TO 7%	6	12	32	45
ABOVE 7%	8	29	42	63

NOTES:
1. DATA SOURCE: MUTUAL FUND FORECASTER NEWSLETTER SPECIAL BONUS REPORT, DATED SEPTEMBER 16, 1987.

APPENDIX C: MKTIME MODEL MTM3

INTRODUCTION

Mktime model MTM3 employs three mktime indicators plus the S&P 500 dividend yield (used in the MTM2 model) to generate Buy and Sell signals. Two of the additional indicators are based upon the 39-week moving averages.

The moving-average market timing concept is a simple concept; namely, that a moving average (over a comparatively long time period; e.g. 39 weeks) of the value of a major market index or of the next asset value of a diversified stock mutual fund indicates long term trends. A rising market is indicated when the moving average has passed through a **minimum value.**

A falling market is indicated when the moving average has passed through a **maximum value.** A 39-week moving average is employed because its value changes slowly and smoothly with time. It does not fluctuate widely in both directions as does a daily or weekly plot of an index or indicator.

MKTIME INDICATORS

The MTM3 mktime model employs four mktime indicators, as follows:

- 39-week moving average (39WMA) of the OTCI (Over-the-Counter Industrial) Index value.
- 39WMA of the top-performing growth fund net asset value.
- Growth mutual fund excess cash holdings as expressed by an Excess Cash Timing Index published by the Mutual Fund Forecaster newsletter.
- S&P 500 dividend yield

MKT3 MARKET TIMING SIGNALS

The MTM3 mktime model generates three types of signals, as follows:

- BUY SIGNAL. Switch all assets from a money market fund to the selected top-performing growth fund.
- TRANSFER SIGNAL. Switch a fraction of growth fund assets to a money market fund.
- BUY CONFIRM SIGNAL. Switch previously transferred assets from a money market fund to the selected top-performing growth fund.
- SELL SIGNAL. Switch all assets from the growth fund to a money market fund.

39WMA SIGNAL GENERATION CRITERIA

BUY SIGNAL GENERATION CRITERIA
A Buy signal is generated when:

The 39WMA is falling rapidly towards a minimum value, and

The current indicator value rises rapidly so as to cross its 39WMA.

BUY CONFIRM SIGNAL GENERATION CRITERIA

A Buy Confirm signal is generated when the 39WMA plot of a market timing indicator (in a Buy mktime status) flattens out and then resumes its upward path. In other words, the 39WMA does NOT pass through a maximum value and does NOT generate a Sell signal. Such a signal was generated by the OTCI indicator on January 9, 1976. The specific criteria for generation of a Buy Confirm signal are:

- The current indicator value has previously crossed below the 39WMA but a Sell signal was NOT generated. (See the following paragraph for Sell signal generation criteria).
- The current indicator value reverses its course and crosses above the 39WMA. The Buy Confirm signal is generated when the second 39WMA crossover occurs.

SELL SIGNAL GENERATION CRITERIA

A sell signal is generated when the 39WMA passes through a maximum value. The OTCI mktime indicator generated a Sell signal on August 21, 1981.

The specific criteria for generation of a Sell signal are:

- The current indicator value has previously crossed below the 39WMA. For example, the current OTCI indicator value crossed below its 39WMA on July 3, 1981.

and

- The current indicator value falls below and remains below (for at least two weeks) its value 39 weeks ago. These events occurred on August 14/21, 1981.
  The Sell signal was generated on the second week that the current indicator value was below its value 39 weeks ago; i.e. on August 21, 1981.

EXCESS-CASH TIMING INDEX SIGNAL GENERATION CRITERIA

This index is based upon the average percentage of the total portfolio assets of all U.S. growth funds that is invested in cash equivalents.

The index measures the difference between the actual cash/assets percentage and a "normal" cash/assets percentage.

The "normal" cash/assets percentage is defined as the sum of (1) 4% of the growth funds total assets and (2) an amount slightly more than 1/2 the commercial paper rate of return.

For example, if the commercial paper rate of return is 9%, the "normal" cash/assets percentage is equal to 8.5% (4 + 9/2). If the actual cash/assets percentage is 10%, then the Excess-Cash Timing Index is 1.5%. This index is published monthly in the *Mutual Fund Forecaster* newsletter.

Positive index values (which reflect excess cash holdings by U.S. growth mutual funds) are bullish and would validate a Buy signal generated by another indicator.

On the other hand, negative index values are bearish and would validate a Sell signal generated by another indicator. A zero index value is neutral.

S&P 500 DIVIDEND YIELD SIGNAL GENERATION CRITERIA

The signal generation criteria for this indicator are described in Appendix B.

TRANSFER SIGNAL GENERATION CRITERIA

When the growth fund return (GFR) during a Buy cycle reaches or exceeds a specified threshold percentage, 30% of the growth fund's assets are transferred to a money market fund.

The threshold percentage is equal to (25 + D) where D depends upon the number of previous Buy cycles in the Buy period as shown in Table 62.

The notes in Table 62 provide a definition of three terms: (1) Buy period, (2) Buy cycle and (3) threshold returns.

Thus, in the second Buy cycle sequence (shown in Table 62) of a Buy period, 30% of the growth fund's assets will be transferred to a money market fund when GFR (growth fund return) reaches or exceeds 25%.

If and when GFR reaches or exceeds the second threshold percentage; i.e. 40% (25% + 15%), an additional 30% of the growth fund's remaining assets will be transferred to the money market fund.

This process is continued until a Buy Confirm or Sell signal is generated.

When a Buy Confirm signal is generated, all money market fund assets are transferred to the selected growth fund.

When a Sell signal is generated, all of the growth fund's remaining assets are transferred to the money market fund

TABLE 62
MKTIME MODEL MTM3
ASSET ALLOCATION THRESHOLD PERCENTAGES VS BUY CYCLE SEQUENCE NUMBER

BUY CYCLE SEQUENCE NUMBER [1]	D VALUE	THRESHOLD NUMBER [NOTE 2]				
		#1	#2	#3	#4	#%
1	20	25	45	65	85	105
2	15	25	40	55	70	85
3	10	25	35	45	55	65
4	5	25	30	35	40	45
5	5	25	30	35	40	45

NOTES:
1. A BUY PERIOD IS THE TIME PERIOD BETWEEN A BUY SIGNAL AND THE NEXT SELL SIGNAL. THERE ARE ONE OR MORE BUY CYCLES IN A BUY PERIOD. THESE CYCLES ARE IDENTIFIED BY A SEQUENCE NUMBER.
2. DURING A BUY CYCLE, THE GROWTH FUND RETURN MAY REACH OR EXCEED ONE OR MORE PERCENTAGE THRESHOLDS. THESE THRESHOLDS ARE IDENTIFIED BY NUMBER.
3. THE THRESHOLD PERCENTAGE FOR THRESHOLDS #2 AND ABOVE VARIES WITH THE D VALUE. IT IS EQUAL TO 25+D, 25+2D, 25+3D, ETC.

MTM3 MKTIME MODEL SIGNAL GENERATION CRITERIA

BUY SIGNAL GENERATION CRITERIA

A Buy signal is generated when:

The S&P 500 Dividend Yield is in a Buy status
and
At least two of the other three indicators generate or have generated Buy signals.

SELL SIGNAL GENERATION CRITERIA

A Sell signal is generated when:

The S&P 500 Dividend Yield indicator generates a Sell signal

or

At least two of the other three indicators generate or have generated Sell signals.

BUY CONFIRM SIGNAL GENERATION CRITERIA

A Buy Confirm signal is generated when:

The S&P 500 Dividend Yield indicator is in a Buy status

and

One of the 39WMA indicators generates a Buy Confirm signal

and

At least one of the other two indicators is in a Buy status.

MTM3 HYPOTHETICAL PERFORMANCE RESULTS

During the 11-year period from 1982 through 1992, the S&P 500 Index achieved an 11-year MAR of 19% when MTM3-timed as compared to 16.7% when bought and held.

APPENDIX D: MKTIME MODEL MTM4

INTRODUCTION

Mktime Model MTM4 employs the seasonality market timing approach. This market timing model was developed in the early 1970's at the Institute of econometric Research on the basis of an exhaustive analysis of daily stock price returns extending back to 1927. The Institute publishes two investment newsletters (Mutual Fund Forecaster and Market Logic) which have been describing this market timing model and its performance.

MTM4 MKTIME INDICATORS

The MTM4 mktime model employs two seasonality mktime indicators: (1) end-of-month and (2) pre-holiday.

The **end-of-month** mktime indicator generates a Buy signal on the day before the last trading day of the month and a Sell signal on the fourth trading day of the next month with one exception. If the fourth trading day is a Monday (or the first trading day of the week), then a Sell signal is generated on the fifth day (Tuesday) (or the second trading day of the week). This indicator is based on the fact that stocks have a marked tendency to rise on the last trading day of every month during the first four trading days of every month. This continuous span of five or six days constitutes the end-of-month seasonality indicator. Several reasons may exist for this unusual phenomenon including month-end portfolio adjustments by institutions; investment of monthly stock-purchase-plan proceeds by mutual funds; and month-end salary draws by members of the investing public which route them into various investments.

The **pre-holiday** mktime indicator generates a Buy signal on the third trading day preceding a stock exchange holiday and a Sell signal on the trading day preceding the holiday. This indicator is based on the fact that stocks also show a definite tendency to rise in each of the two trading days preceding market holiday closings. The most likely explanation for this bullish, pre-holiday propensity is that stock traders wish to lighten up on the short side of their portfolio (i.e. buy stocks which they have shorted) just prior to the holiday in order to protect themselves from any unexpected good news that develops when the market is closed.

1993 MTM4 IMPLEMENTATION

Tables 63A and 63B list the MTM4 1993 Buy/Sell transaction dates which result from the application of the above described rules for each of the two MTM4 mktime indicators.

MTM4 HYPOTHETICAL PERFORMANCE RESULTS

As shown in Chapter 6, the performance of the MTM4-timed S&P 500 Index differed markedly during the first and second 5-year period of the 11-year period from 1982 to 1992 as indicated in the following table:

PERIOD	S&P 500 MEAN ANNUALIZED RETURNS %	
1982-1986	19.9	10.6
1987-1991	15.4	25.3
1988-1992	15.9	22.0

TABLE 63A
MKTIME MODEL MTM4 (SEASONALITY)
1993 BUY/SELL TRANSACTION DATES

TYPE FUND	EXECUTION DATES		APPLICABLE MKTIME INDICATOR
	BUY	SELL	
GROWTH	12/31/92	1/06/93	END-OF-MONTH
MONEY MARKET	1/06	1/28	
GROWTH	1/28	2/04	END-OF-MONTH
MONEY MARKET	2/04	2/10	
GROWTH	2/10	2/12	PRE-HOLIDAY
MONEY MARKET	2/12	2/25	
GROWTH	2/25	3/04	END-OF-MONTH
MONEY MARKET	3/04	3/30	
GROWTH	3/30	4/08	END-OF-MONTH PLUS
MONEY MARKET	4/08	4/29	PRE-HOLIDAY
GROWTH	4/29	5/06	END-OF-MONTH
MONEY MARKET	5/06	5/26	
GROWTH	5/26	6/04	PRE-HOLIDAY PLUS
MONEY MARKET	6/04	6/29	END-OF-MONTH

TABLE 63B
MKTIME MODEL MTM4 (SEASONALITY)
1993 BUY SELL TRANSACTION DATES

TYPE FUND	EXECUTION DATES		APPLICABLE MKTIME INDICATOR
	BUY	SELL	
GROWTH	6/29	7/07	END-OF-MONTH
MONEY MARKET	7/07	7/29	OVERLAPPING
			PRE-HOLIDAY
GROWTH	7/29	8/05	END-OF-MONTH
MONEY MARKET	8/05	8/30	
GROWTH	8/30	9/08	END-OF-MONTH
MONEY MARKET	9/08	9/29	OVERLAPPING
			PRE-HOLIDAY
GROWTH	9/29	10/06	END-OF-MONTH
MONEY MARKET	10/06	10/28	
GROWTH	10/28	11/04	END-OF-MONTH
MONEY MARKET	11/04	11/22	
GROWTH	11/22	12/07	PRE-HOLIDAY PLUS
MONEY MARKET	12/07	12/21	END-OF-MONTH
GROWTH	12/21	12/31	PRE-HOLIDAY PLUS END-OF-MONTH

APPENDIX E: MKTIME MODEL MTM5

INTRODUCTION

Mktime Model MTM5 employs software (used on a personal computer) provided by AIQ, Inc. and known as *Market Expert* Version 3.51. This market timing system is an artificial intelligence-based expert system. An expert system is a software program that contains the knowledge of experts on a particular subject and is able to use this knowledge to help make decisions and solve problems. As an expert system, *MarketExpert* consists of a knowledge base and an inference engine. Knowledge, in the form of rules, is stored in the knowledge base. The inference engine is the thinking component of the expert system.

The rules in the *MarketExpert* knowledge base operate on facts embodied in the technical indicators. These rules are derived from the knowledge of many experts in stock market action and market timing. The technical indicators are computed from daily price, volume and breadth data from three indices: (1) Dow-Jones Industrial Average (DJIA), (2) New York Stock Exchange (NYSE) Index and (3) S&P 500 Index. These rules are combined into a higher level known as Expert Ratings.

The second part of *MarketExpert*, the inference engine, combines the rules in order to determine the Expert Ratings. Each rule is given an assigned value. The weighted total of all rules is normalized to determine the Expert Rating.

The price action of the DJIA is used as the basis of MarketExpert for several reasons:

- It is the universally accepted measure of the market's overall performance.
- There is a significant spread between the high, low and close prices of the DJIA. Such a spread is not seen as often in the other indices.

TECHNICAL INDICATORS

MarketExpert uses 30 technical indicators to generate Expert Ratings. Twenty-four (24) of these indicators are displayed with the Index Plots function of *MarketExpert*. The Index Plot displays the variation during the past 145 days of one of the three indices plus a selected technical indicator. The 24 indicators which are displayed are:

Set #1 Indicators

- Price Phase Indicator
- Volume
- 21-day Volume Accumulation Percentage
- 21-day On-Balance Volume Percentage
- Advance/Decline Oscillator
- Advance/Decline Line
- 21-day Stochastic
- Average Directional Movement
- Money Flow Index
- High/Low Indicator
- Relative Strength, S&P 500 Index
- Zoom

Set #2 Indicators

- Moving Average Convergence-Divergence Index (MACDI)
- Volume Oscillator
- Accumulation/Distribution
- On-Balance Volume
- Summation Index
- Traders Index
- SK-SD Stochastics
- Directional Movement Index (DMI)
- Positive Volume Index
- Negative Volume Index
- Relative Strength, New York Stock Exchange Index
- Zig Zag

MKTIME MODEL USAGE

Daily Data Input

Seventeen (17) data items are entered daily either manually (from the Wall Street Journal) or electronically (via a wire service). The input data consists of:

- Intraday high, low and close prices of the DJIA, NYSE Index and S&P 500 Index.
- NYSE number of advancing issues and total volume of advancing stocks.
- NYSE number of declining issues and total volume of declining stocks.
- NYSE number of unchanged issues and total volume of the unchanged stocks.
- Number of NYSE issues that reached new highs.
- Number of NYSE issues that reached new lows.

Daily Data Output

Two Expert Ratings are shown in the lower right corner of the Index Plots for the current market date. Expert ratings between 95 and 100 indicate that an unconfirmed signal has been generated.

The sum of the two ratings is approximately 100. An unconfirmed Buy signal is generated when the left hand rating is between 95 and 100. An unconfirmed Sell signal is generated when the right hand rating is between 95 and 100.

The price phase indicator (shown as "Phase" in the right hand corner of the Index Plots) is used to confirm an expert rating. A Buy signal is confirmed when the change in the price phase indicator from the previous day is positive.

A Sell signal is confirmed when the change in the price phase indicator from the previous day is negative. An Expert Rating may be confirmed within a 5-day period after a Buy or Sell signal is generated.

MTM5 HYPOTHETICAL PERFORMANCE RESULTS

The GFSS2-selected top fund when timed by the MTM5 mktime model achieved a mean annualized return of 31.5% during the 11-year period from 1982 through 1992 (see Table 45). During the same period, the S&P 500 Index achieved a mean annualized return of 16.7%.

APPENDIX F: MKTIME MODEL MTM6

INTRODUCTION

Mktime model MTM6 employs the MTM5 mktime model (AIQ MarketExpert 3.51) in conjunction with the MTM4 (seasonality) end-of-month indicator. If the MTM5 model is in a Sell status on the next-to-last trading day of the month, then MTM6 generates a Buy signal and remains in a Buy status for five days (last trading day of the month plus the first four trading days of the next month). This Buy period is extended under the conditions described in Appendix D for the MTM4 mktime model. The Buy period is foreshortened if MTM5 generates a Sell signal during the 5-day period.

MTM6 HYPOTHETICAL PERFORMANCE RESULTS

The GFSS2-selected top fund when timed by the MTM6 mktime model achieved a mean annualized return of 38.3% during the 11-year period from 1982 through 1992. During the same period, the S&P 500 Index achieved a mean annualized return of 16.7%.

APPENDIX G: MUTUAL FUND TRADING FEES

INTRODUCTION

Many mutual funds limit the number of asset switches or transfers (from one fund to another in the same family of funds) made per year by an investor. The usual limit is four switches per year. Moreover, switching from one fund family to another is time consuming; i.e. such transfers usually cannot be executed by a telephone call within one day.

In order to implement the two top-performing investment systems that are described in this report, it is neçessary to (1) effect 10 to 12 switches per year and (2) switch assets from one fund family to another by telephone. These actions can be implemented via a mutual fund trading broker. At the present time (January 1993), there are three well-known mutual fund trading brokers: Charles Schwab & Co., Jack White & Co. and Waterhouse Securities, Inc. Our analysis of their transaction fee schedules indicates that Jack White & Co. has the lowest fees per mutual fund switch. Jack White & Co. (800-233-3411) handles accounts for individual investors. Shareholder Services Corporation (800-582-8585) is a subsidiary of Jack White & Co. that handles institutional accounts. The trading fees as a function of the amount transferred are shown in the following table:

MUTUAL FUND TRADING FEES PER SWITCH				
Market Value Transfered	Jack White & Company		Shareholders Services Corp.	
	FEE*	% Mkt Value	FEE*	% Mkt Value
$10,000	$40	0.40	$30	0.30
$20,000	$60	0.30	$40	0.20
$30,000	$80	0.27	$50	0.16
$40,000	$100	0.25	$60	0.15
$50,000	$85	0.17	$60	0.12
$100,000	$135	0.14	$85	0.09

* minimum FEE IS $29

The above fees are based upon the following formulas:

AMOUNT TRANSFERRED	JACK WHITE & CO.	SHAREHOLDERS SERVICES CORP.
less than $50,000	$20 + 0.002 x A	$20 + 0.001 x A
greater than $50,000	$35 + 0.001 x A	$35 + 0.0005 x A

where A is the amount transferred.

APPENDIX H: BIBLIOGRAPHY

Hulbert Financial Digest , 316 Commerce Street, Alexandria, VA 22314 (703-683-5905).

MarketExpert Software [manual], AIQ, Inc., P.O. Drawer 7530, Incline Village, NV 89450 (800-332-2999).

MoniResearch Newsletter, P.O. Box 19146, Portland, OR 97280 (503-625-6716).

Mutual Fund Forecaster Newsletter, The Institute for Econometric Research, 3471 North Federal, Fort Lauderdale, FL 33306 (800-442-9000).

SOURCE: The Complete Guide to Investment Information, Jae K. Shim and Joel G. Siegle, International Publishing Corporation, Chicago, IL.

Index

F

G

H

I

S

T

V

W

BECOME PART OF THE

Association of Mutual Fund Investors

(AMFI)

AMFI OBJECTIVE:

AMFI strives to assist its members to become effective managers of their own assets via mutual fund investments by conducting programs of research, education, and information dissemination. Such programs emphasize the QUANTITATIVE evaluation of alternative sources of mutual fund information and advice.

For more information about the Association of Mutual Fund Investors or for a membership application, please write:

ASSOCIATION OF MUTUAL FUND INVESTORS
1045 BUSLETON PIKE, SUITE 365
FEASTERVILLE, PA 19053

The authors, Aaron and David Coleman, can be reached at the above address.

The Association of Mutual Fund Investors (AMFI) is not affiliated in any way with International Information Associates, Inc.
Please contact AMFI regarding membership information, and IIAI for information on this book.

THE BUSINESS-EDUCATION PARTNERSHIP
ARTHUR G. SHARP & ELIZABETH O. SHARP

ISBN 0-945510-10-1, 251 pages

*BUSINESS-ONE IRWIN NO:11-4063-01

$12.95

This book describes how companies and educators can work together to ensure that tomorrow's workers have the skills necessary for success. The authors show how to take advantage of programs available to ensure a steady supply of talented workers, and how to enhance the relationship between business and academia. For education administrators, executives, corporate trainers, government officials, and faculty members in business and education programs. Being translated into Portuguese.

"Every educator in the country should have a copy of this book, and be required to study it." Virginia Sink, The Tribune [OK]

"...a detailed strategic plan for improving the system of education...the book consumes over 250 pages and everyome holds a clue to success..." The Bookreader Magazine

"The backgrounds of this husband and wife team make them uniquely qualified to write this book. If you are looking for a good book...THE BUSINESS-EDUCATION PARTNERSHIP may fit the bill." D.Williamson, The Rocky Hill [CT] Post.

AMERICAN CHAMPIONS:
A HISTORY OF BUSINESS SUCCESS

ARTHUR G. SHARP

ISBN 0-945510-09-8, 410 pages

$ 17.95

American Champions relates the history of 13 American companies founded between 1711 and 1890, ***and still independent and profitable today***. Mr. Sharp has done a great deal of research into the lives of these companies and ties it all together to show how today's companies can use the lessons learned from the champions to prosper and grow in today's world. Contains historical photographs. *The Bookreader*, a California based review magazine has called this book: " ...good advice, ...sound depictions, ...an excellence sourcebook."

ABOUT THE AUTHOR:

Arthur G. Sharp is a noted business and historical writer. He is the author of five business books, and hundreds of articles on business and education topics. Mr. Sharp, formerly Manager of Personnel Communications for a large insurance company is now on the business faculty of Central Connecticut State University.

International Information Associates, Inc.
P.O. Box 773
Morrisville, PA 19067
800-645-6973

LESSONS FROM THE BEST MANAGERS:

SIMPLE AND PROVEN TECHNIQUES THAT PRODUCE BIG RESULTS

PAUL B. THORNTON

ISBN 0-945510-07-1 $ 12.95 123 PAGES, ILLUSTRATED

"If you're a new manager, [Lessons] will save you a lot of blood, sweat and tears ... even if you've been around the block ... a little refresher course may be just what you need to renew the faith." — *Personal Selling Power Magazine*

"A useful group of readings for managers. The author's advice to managers squares with the major research in the field." — *Prof. A. Peter Mattaliano, The Hartford Graduate Center*

"Managers who have to put plans into action must present these plans in a clear, concise understandable manner. *Lessons from the Best Managers* provides this information in a fast-paced, easy-to-understand manner." — *T.J. McCann, Executive Director, Toastmasters International*

International Information Associates, Inc.
P.O. Box 773
Morrisville, PA 19067
800-645-6973

PROBING THE MIND OF A SERIAL KILLER
JACK A. APSCHE
FOREWORD BY A. CHARLES PERUTO, JR. ESQ.

ISBN 0-945510-12-8, 223 pages

$11.95

A psychology/law text that will create a revolution in psychological diagnosis, the law, and law enforcement. Contains never before published letters and drawings by convicted serial killers Gary Heidnik and Harrison Marty Graham.

"This book begins the discovery of the inner world of the serial killer. To understand this in the detail presented by Jack Apsche ... can help society more than all the death penalties and life in prison sentences ever can." A. Charles Peruto, Jr, Noted Defense Attorney.

"I would recommend this book to law enforcement personnel, attorneys, and all those persons interested in the mindset of those who commit serial murders. These comments are based on 23 years of police experience and 16 years as a homicide investigator for the city of Philadelphia." Lamont Anderson, Private Investigator

"... as accurate as the clock on the wall of the Hall of Justice." Joel Moldovsy, Defense Attorney

International Information Associates, Inc.
P.O. Box 773
Morrisville, PA 19067
800-645-6973

TAMING THE DRAGON PART 1: WORKING WITH TAIWAN

CRAIG T. SANTY

ISBN 0-945510-16-0, DECEMBER 1993

$ 16.95

An excellent hands-on workbook, and guide for all foreign businesspeople who wish to do business in or with Taiwan. Presents important and detailed information in a concise easy-to-use manner. It provides the exact names, addresses and offices with which you must work. Includes detailed statistics, graphs, history, forecasts, and other data that businessmen need on a day to day basis. It includes the latest government data, laws, and pending legislation.

Craig Santy has studied literature and writing at the prestigious Interlochen Arts Academy in Michigan. He has a Bachelor's degree in Asian Studies from the University of California at Irvine and a Masters in Journalism from Columbia University's Graduate School of Journalism. Mr. Santy is a consultant for major US and Asian firms and spends much of his time traveling between the US and Taiwan. He does extensive work with the Asian Research Facility (Cerritos, CA) in improving relations between American and Taiwanese business.

International Information Associates, Inc.
P.O. Box 773
Morrisville, PA 19067
800-645-6973

TAMING THE DRAGON PART 2:
WORKING WITH CHINA

WEN JINHAI

ISBN 0-945510-17-9, DECEMBER 1993

$16.95

The People's Republic of China, with a population of 1.3 billion, represents an enormous market for all foreign business. Since 1979, China has been implementing an open-door policy to the outside world as it develops its own unique position in the global business village.

An excellent hands-on workbook, and guide for all foreign businesspeople who wish to do business in or with The People's Republic of China. Presents important and practical information in a concise easy-to-use manner. Unlike many other titles on China this book not only gives an explanation of the laws, regulations on investments, and taxes but offers a unique look at China itself, including its consumer market.

Wen Jinhai is a graduate of Xiamen University in Fujian Province where he was born. He was formerly employed at the Civil Aviation Administration in Beijing where his study of China's airports gave him a unique perspective of Chinese communication and allowed him to visit most of China's provinces. Wen Jinhai is now Editor of the influential Beijing newspaper "Literature and Art News." He has published many articles about China and its culture and several books, including a novel entitled "Chuang-Hei-Do" relating the social problem of abducted women in China. This book was serialized by the "International Daily News" in Los Angeles in 1991.

.International Information Associates, Inc.
P.O. Box 773
Morrisville, PA 19067
800-645-6973

HOW TO HIRE WINNERS — LEGALLY

LAURENCE LIPSETT

ISBN 0-945510-20-9, JUNE 1994

$ 17.95

This book fills a critical need of human resource practitioners for effective staffing techniques that avoid the pitfalls of the Civil Rights Act of 1991 and other laws that affect hiring. Explains in details the do's and don'ts for recruiting, application forms, interviews, reference checking, physical examinations, and drug testing. The author also demystifies psychological testing and offers legal and effective alternatives. A list of 29 applicant databases helps expand recruiting horizons. Interview excerpts from real applicants show how to identify strong applicants, weak applicants and impostors. This book is a practical updated guide for recruiting and selecting.

Laurence Lipsett is a consulting industrial psychologist specializing in personnel selection. He has consulted with more than 200 firms including Xerox, Bausch & Lomb, Quaker Oats, and Corning, Inc. Dr. Lipsett earned a bachelor's degree from the University of Michigan and a master's and doctor's degree from the University of Buffalo. Before he began his private practice, he was director of a community psychological services center at Rochester Institute of Technology, adjunct professor at the University of Rochester and Alfred University, and Professor of Industrial Psychology at Empire State College. Recipient of the 1987 State University of New York Chancellor's Award for Excellence in Teaching, Dr. Lipsett is the author of more than 40 articles in professional journals, and is the senior author of *Personnel Selection and Recruitment* published by Allyn and Bacon. Dr. Lipsett lives in Webster, NY where he is a licensed psychologist and Diplomate of the American Board of Professional Psychology.

International Information Associates, Inc.
P.O. Box 773
Morrisville, PA 19067
800-645-6973

TOTAL QUALITY LEADERSHIP:
A TRAINING APPROACH
JOSEPH L. PICOGNA

ISBN 0-945510-15-2 September 1993

$ 17.95

Covers training and program development as it relates to a comprehensive program for the development of a quality conscious organization. Includes a highly interactive set of learning experiences designed to prepare the reader to design, deliver and implement a program. Also designed to be used as a one semester course in training from a systems perspective.

The author adjunct Professor of Organizational Behavior at Temple University School of Business and Management, and the Principal of Joseph Picogna Associates, a management consulting firm. The author has an MBA from the US Navy Post Graduate School, and an Ed.D. from Temple University. He is a member of the American Management Association, Society for Human Resource Management, American Society for Training & Development and the American Educational Research Association.

International Information Associates, Inc.
P.O. Box 773
Morrisville, PA 19067
800-645-6973

THE RISING SUN ON MAIN STREET: WORKING WITH THE JAPANESE REVISED 2ND EDITION

ALISON R. LANIER

ISBN 0-945510-11-X Irwin title # 11-4062-02, 1992 $12.95

Authorized Japanese edition by Yohan Publications, Tokyo; translated to Spanish and Portuguese by Legis, S.A. Bogota.

267 pages, appendixes, $12.95

" ... describes ways Japanese differ from westerners, Japan as a superpower ... relations with various other countries. Recommended reading list." — David Rouse, ALA Booklist.

"...I have read many books offering advice on understanding and dealing with the Japanese, and how they see us. This book of essential insights is the best ... a close reading of this well-written book will be essential to success." — Melvin A. Conant, Editor & Publisher, Geopolitics & Energy

"Lanier knows and relates her knowledge without fanfare. You listen to this expert. Invaluable as a straight-talking, practical guide to the Japanese." — The Bookreader Magazine

" ... provided meaningful insights. American managers need to read a book such as The Rising Sun on Main Street." — G.E. Gomolski, Vice President, Chrysler Motors Corporation.

"This is a book of great value for any Americans (or other foreign nationals too, for that matter) engaged in business with the Japanese ... in Japan, in the US, or in any other part of the world. Japanese culture is carefully explored; points of difference carefully explained ... a sound and readable paperback." — W.G. Downs, Associate Director, Rockefeller Foundation

" ...useful whatever your business relationship [with the Japanese] may be." — Washington Researchers Publishing

"Interesting and excellent book, useful for college exchange students as well as business and government." John E. Sawyer, former President, Williams College, MA.

International Information Associates, Inc.
P.O. Box 773
Morrisville, PA 19067
800-645-6973